Exact Change

Exact Change

And Other Plays

by

David Epstein

Retriever Press
AN IMPRINT OF RIVERTOWNS BOOKS

Copyright © 2026 by David Epstein. All rights reserved.

No part of this book may be used or reproduced by any means, graphic, electronic, or mechanical, including photocopying, recording, taping, or by any information storage retrieval system without the written permission of the publisher, except in the case of brief quotations embodied in critical articles and reviews.

This book is human authored.

NO AI TRAINING: Without in any way limiting the author's and publisher's exclusive rights under copyright, any use of this publication to train generative artificial intelligence (AI) technologies to generate text is expressly prohibited. The author reserves all rights to license uses of this work for generative AI training and development of machine learning language models.

"Exact Change" was published in 2000 in an acting edition by Dramatists Play Service, Inc. Copyright 2000 by David Epstein, all rights reserved.

Paperback edition ISBN-13: 978-1-953943-80-4
Electronic edition ISBN-13: 978-1-953943-81-1

LCCN Imprint Name: Retriever Press
Library of Congress Control Number: 2026935864

Retriever Press is an imprint of Rivertowns Books. Copies of this book are available from all bookstores, other stores that carry books, and online retailers. Requests for information and other correspondence may be addressed to:

> Retriever Press
> 240 Locust Lane
> Irvington NY 10533
> Info@rivertownsbooks.com

For Kate

Contents

Preface	5
Exact Change	7
Hair of the Dog	137
Shades	259
Acknowledgments	365
About the Author	367

Preface

JACQUES LEVY directed the first version of *Exact Change* at Yale's Winter Fest, another version at the McCarter Theatre in Princeton, then (following critically acclaimed productions in Chicago and London), in New York, the version included here. A force in the New York theatre (*America Hurrah, Scuba Duba, Oh, Calcutta! Sam Shepard's Geography of a Horse Dreamer*, and more), he was my great friend.

Shades was first produced at South Coast Rep in Costa Mesa, California. When I reread the play, it demanded a contemporary rewrite. The new *Shades* it included here.

Hair of the Dog is ready to get up on its feet. I'm hopeful it will be barking somewhere before long.

December 2025,
Kailua, Hawaii

EXACT CHANGE

EXACT CHANGE

was produced by Thomas J. Schwarz and Ellen Howe in New York City on June 1, 1999. It was directed by Jacques Levy; the set design was by Ray Recht; the lighting design was by Chris Dallos; the costume design was by Tina Firestone, and the stage manager was James Beaumont. The cast was as follows:

Botts	Geoff Pierson
Bompkee	Ken Ryan
Merola	Charles Stransky

The play was produced by The Mandrake Theatre Company (Aaron Mullen and Steven O'Shea, founders) at the Lyric Hammersmith Theatre in London, England, on October 21, 1993. It was directed by Aaron Mullen; the set design was by Tom Pye; the lighting design was by Michael Calf; the sound design was by Matt McKenzie, and the stage manager was Nicole Griffiths. The cast was as follows:

Botts	Kevin McNally
Bompkee	Mike McShane
Merola	Steven O'Shea

ACT ONE

The lights come up. A beautifully burnished mahogany bar, with a mirror behind it, is up center, angled. There are a few circular tables with chairs stacked on top of them. A door to the right of the bar heads into the kitchen and another to the bathroom, up right. An entrance is down left.

We hear the jiggling of a lock and BOMPKEE, wearing a down jacket, rushes in. He drops a newspaper on the bar, and leans against it for a moment breathing hard.

MEROLA, in a long leather overcoat, comes in after him, switching on the lights.

Bompkee hurries off right to the bathroom.

Merola yanks off his overcoat and goes behind the bar. He turns the water on at the sink.

MEROLA
Do you believe this?
          (distressed)
Unheard of! This happens to *no one*. Would you look at this coat. All over the fuckin' coat?
          (starts to scrub the coat, calls out—)
Whatta you know about stains? Is water good? Is that okay with leather?
          (pause)
Is it chemical? You think there's an interaction with that?

(pause)

Hey, you okay in there?

(scrubs)

Sonofabitch!

(pause)

What about soap? Should I try soap?

(thinks)

Soap can't be good on leather. You don't wash leather gloves with soap. Why would you wash a leather coat? Soap kills leather.

(scrubs)

Hey, I think it's comin' out. This is comin' out.

(a toilet flushes)

The tone could be changin' here. Shit. Maybe I scrubbed too hard. Goddammit, sonofabitch!

Bompkee returns wiping his mouth with a napkin.

BOMPKEE

Wait'll it dries.

MEROLA

What?

BOMPKEE

Then look. You can't tell when it's wet. Leather shifts.

MEROLA

(turns off the water, comes forward)

Then what? Suppose it's fucked up? I'll sue his *estate*, that asshole.

                    BOMPKEE
                     (sits)
You take it to a place.

                    MEROLA
What "a place?"

                    BOMPKEE
A specialty place. That's all they do. They specialize.

                    MEROLA
In stains?

                    BOMPKEE
In leather. *Removal.*

                    MEROLA
Blood?

                    BOMPKEE
Ink. Blood. Cum. Whatever.

                    MEROLA
                    (pause)
Okay. That's it. They'll charge a fortune. So what? I love the coat. That's what counts, right? It's an investment. A coat like this, ten, fifteen years, it appreciates. You can't buy good, old leather coats anymore. They're prohibitive.
                    (pause)
Maybe a slight stain is unique. You never know. We'll see how it comes out. It could be distinctive.

(looks at him)
You didn't get any?

                BOMPKEE
                (a shrug)
You were on the outside.

                MEROLA

My luck.
                (pause)
By your sock. Above. There's a little. Not too bad.
                (pause)
You gave up your breakfast?

    Bompkee nods.

                MEROLA
                (smiles)
Dinner too?

                BOMPKEE
Felt like the whole week.

    Bompkee begins to take the chairs down from the tables and off the bar.

                MEROLA
You believe it? On a Sunday? We're walkin' along—

                BOMPKEE
What's the difference what day?

MEROLA

I don't know. It's an intangible. Somehow I don't associate suicide with a Sunday. It usually has more of a business ring to it.

(pause)

He fucks up at the office Friday, brings it home with him, broods—I suppose.

(pause)

Sold when he shouldda bought. Put when he shouldda held. Said No to an obvious Yes. Saw profits dematerialize overnight. Can't face the Monday options, the Tuesday quotes. He opens the window.

(considers)

A lotta guys in bonds are unhappy.

BOMPKEE

(starts to put tablecloths on the tables)

You know it couldda been personal. Sunday can be a downer. All alone, no family. Wife left him. A cuppa coffee, nothin' to do, high up—

MEROLA

How do you know his wife left him? That's pure speculation.

(shakes his head)

Besides, this guy was in a suit. Pin-stripes.

BOMPKEE

So?

MEROLA

You don't get dressed up to jump out a window.

BOMPKEE

He mightta been somewhere. Earlier.

Look at each other, nod.

BOMPKEE AND MEROLA

Church.

Merola reads the newspaper.

BOMPKEE

You know I can't help thinkin' somethin' about this guy looks familiar.

MEROLA

Familiar? This guy? There were no features. It was a total obliteration. Mr. Sidewalk meets Mr. Face. We're starin' at meatballs, a little tomato sauce.

BOMPKEE

I know that!

MEROLA

So what couldda been familiar? Maybe somethin' you ate?

Bompkee puts out ketchup bottles, salt and pepper.

BOMPKEE

Where the hell's Ritchie? We got people comin'.

MEROLA
He'll be here. He gets ten minutes grace for bein' engaged.

BOMPKEE
This Maureen's already got his balls wrapped around her finger. Amazing.

MEROLA
It's nice to see.

BOMPKEE
I never thought it'd happen to Ritchie.

MEROLA
Everybody takes the pipe one time.
(checking out the room)
You know, I think once we get a second place goin' we should re-decorate in here. A fresh motif. A sense of movement. Nothin' static. Maybe ships.

BOMPKEE
We won't be able to afford it.

MEROLA
Money will be no problem.

BOMPKEE
You gonna print it?

MEROLA
Borrow. It's the same thing.

BOMPKEE

We open a second place we could be in over our heads.

MEROLA

You cover your ass as you march forward. How? Should things get tight, suddenly you're under the gun, you ask yourself do we cut back? If so, on what? Quality? Do we begin to water the scotch? Bread the burgers? Fire the help? Step back into operations? Is that feasible? What are our options? Who gives a fuck? Who cares? We care. Our families will care. So what do we do? We proceed forcefully, with caution. Like that.
(pause)
Meanwhile, every opportunity we get, we buy. We invest as little real money as possible for the largest possible return. We leverage our fucking souls! To the hilt. Then we sit back.
(pause)
We haven't come this far to be satisfied here. The exposure is too limited. The upside is all too visible.

BOMPKEE

Who have you been talking to?

MEROLA

I read! I keep my ears open. The world doesn't end within these walls.

BOMPKEE

It's a good place. We've been fortunate.

MEROLA

To start, yes. What makes it good is the possibility of what could make it better. You rest on "good" it runs to shit in five minutes. You think if IBM stuck with making good typewriters they woudda come up with data processing? What about the Japanese? Were they satisfied making good cameras? It led to somethin'. What did it lead to? Chips. Now the whole fucking world is run by chips. Would there be chips if some Jap scientist in glasses hadn't gone that one extra step beyond?

(pause)

If civilization doesn't advance it crumbles. Let's face it, bein' in business is like bein' a shark. Move or die. Period.

BOMPKEE

So how does this account for the successful small-businessman? Tell me that. Not everyone is a Donald Rectoid Trump.

MEROLA

Maybe there is no such thing anymore as the small businessman. Okay. Suppose we didn't go out and buy another place. Do we stand pat? No. We move beyond burgers and bar nuts, into a new concept. Maybe we go into chicken, ribs, exotic drinks, like that. We diversify. Reinvent the fucking wheel each time. That's the challenge. People who accept chance, who dare, those are the winners.

(pause)

What are you shakin' your head about?

BOMPKEE

You can't beat a good hamburger.

Bompkee, behind the bar, cuts up lemons and limes.

MEROLA
(looks at him)
Down the road we could have a real partnership problem on our hands.

He turns and moves away, a pause.

BOMPKEE
So you think Ritchie's gonna go through with this one? Maureen? Will it last?

MEROLA
What "last"? they're engaged, aren't they?

BOMPKEE
And he was engaged to what's-her-name too, remember? The "angel"?

MEROLA
Never bring that up in his presence.

BOMPKEE
No shit.

MEROLA
That girl was an obvious psycho. Her rip cord had been pulled.

BOMPKEE
Apparently.

MEROLA

A born outpatient. Even to the untrained eye, here was an incomplete human being. No head. The head was missing. Absent.

BOMPKEE

And why couldn't he see that?

MEROLA

A man will always choose to see the pretty face and ignore the mashed potatoes behind it. Lucky for all of us the Angel flipped out when she did.

BOMPKEE

He wouldda had a lifetime of agony.

MEROLA

Exactly.

BOMPKEE

The whole thing remains mysterious. Two days before the wedding?
(a pause)

MEROLA

He visits her.

Bompkee looks at him. Merola nods.

In the nuthouse.

BOMPKEE

He *told* you that?

MEROLA

Someone I know. A friend of her family. Once a month. Without fail. He goes.

BOMPKEE

He never mentions it. Her name.

MEROLA

Guys don't chat about their failures. That's a rule of thumb.

BOMPKEE

What "failure"? The girl took sick.

MEROLA

Your fiancé, the chosen woman of your dreams who you have carefully selected to spend your life with, flips out. What is that, a *success*?

BOMPKEE

How did such a thing happen? One night, just like that she's in the stratosphere?

MEROLA

Chance plays a major role. It's all a gamble. Kids, Marriage. Love. You insert your dick into somethin' warm, you think: This is good, this feels right. Next thing you know, boom, you got a kid with one of those large heads, you know? Or maybe it grows up like you fed it nothin' but lemons, mean and bitter. Or it goes out and creates mayhem, pleads innocent. Or maybe it's just a disappointment, amounts to shit in front of your very eyes and you gotta live to see it.

(pause)

And the great girl you marry? Turns out to be a complainer, chronic, wakes up, complains before she brushes her teeth. Unsatisfiable as a wife, terrific as a girlfriend. Who knew? Or else you hook a sick one, pills lined up on the counter, bedridden, in a housecoat with the hair all over the place. You keep wonderin', "Where's that girl I married? What happened to love? Is this my life?"

BOMPKEE
(disturbed)

It doesn't have to be that way. It's not just luck.

MEROLA
(picks up the paper, the sports pages)

We are who we eat. Risk deep feeling at your own peril.

BOMPKEE

Things alter, they can get better!

MEROLA

It happens.
(pause, reading)
I haven't seen much of Mary lately.

Bompkee looks at him.

She's still workin' for the dentist, am I right?

BOMPKEE
So?

MEROLA
So? She usually drops by, that's all.

BOMPKEE
Is that right?

MEROLA
(looks up)
Hey, it was a simple observation.

BOMPKEE
Have you talked to her?

MEROLA
I just told you I haven't seen her.

BOMPKEE
Have you *talked* to her?

MEROLA
No. I have not talked to Mary recently.

BOMPKEE
Oh, recently? What's that mean?

MEROLA
What's the matter with you? Are you ovulating or somethin'?

BOMPKEE

What "recently"?

MEROLA

To the best of my recollection about a month. How's that?

BOMPKEE

A month?

MEROLA

Right.

BOMPKEE

What was the topic? Was it about me?

MEROLA

What?

BOMPKEE

The conversation. Did it concern me? Her husband.

MEROLA

How do I know?

BOMPKEE

Think.

MEROLA

I shredded all notes from that conversation. What's up your ass, pine cones?

BOMPKEE

No mention of me? The relationship?

MEROLA

The relationship? Am I a *therapist*?

BOMPKEE

Did she accuse me of anything?

Merola looks at him.

Forget it. Forget it!

Merola shrugs, reads.

This party was his goddam idea. Where is he? We pay off the balloon, we celebrate. Who's supposed to do all the settin' up? This is totally typical of his behavior.
(pause)
I didn't get to bed till four a.m., closin' up.
(pause)
I couldda been busy now!

MEROLA

It's always a possibility.

They look at one another, a silence. Merola turns to a new page in the newspaper—does a double take.

What is this?

BOMPKEE
What?

MEROLA
Good shit. Look at this! Look at this.

BOMPKEE
(comes over, checks it out)
Who the fuck took this picture?

MEROLA
Can we assume it was someone with a camera? With fingers! If you get stabbed in the heart do you ask where the knife was made?
(reading)
Arabs? Israelis?—Good shit!

BOMPKEE
"A terrorist plotting haven!" Right next door, the car service? This is a scandal—the neighborhood.
(still looking at the paper)

MEROLA
Whoa. Hold on. A newspaper is a highly visible format. Our place is seen. The entire facade, with the sign, page two. That's free advertising. Remember, "There is no such thing as bad publicity"? Somebody *said* that.

BOMPKEE
I don't think it holds true for restaurants.

MEROLA

This picture could be a boon in disguise.

BOMPKEE

Local Arab assholes plot to blow the balls off an Israeli attaché so interested crowds will suddenly congregate here for *drinks*? We *prosper*?

MEROLA

There's an Arab neighborhood around the corner. A community. They love fanatics. These three guys who are now in jail, they become martyrs. We are in a position to capitalize on it.

BOMPKEE

We encourage the local Arabs.

MEROLA

Exactly.

BOMPKEE

And how do you encourage an Arab? What *tack* do we take? We know virtually nothing about Arabs. For instance, do they drink?

MEROLA

Everybody drinks. It's America.

BOMPKEE

What "everybody"? There are religions that forbid alcohol. I believe Arab might be one of them.

MEROLA

They're *assimilated*. Just like the rest of us. They don't walk around here with *camels*, do they? Their women don't wear veils. They go to our schools. They speak our language. They are no longer primitive.
(pause)
They drink, smoke, snort, and fuck just like the rest of the goddam country, religion or no religion. Only assholes refuse a drink on religious grounds. The pope himself'll take a drink, for chrissake.

BOMPKEE

Not in public.

MEROLA

What are you talkin' about?

BOMPKEE

When have you ever seen a picture of the pope with a drink in his hand?
(pause)
A place fulla Arabs? Is that an advantage? We piss off the Jews.

MEROLA

What Jews? We got no Jews. Jews drink at home. They're scotch drinkers. It's demographic. Everybody worries about the fuckin' Jews—
(Shakes his head.)
Ritchie's gonna love this.

BOMPKEE

Where the hell is he? Why are we always waitin' on him!

(a pause)

MEROLA

Is Ritchie's sister comin' tonight?

BOMPKEE
(surprised)

What?

MEROLA

Jeannie. Is she comin'?

BOMPKEE
(looks at him)

How would I know if his sister is comin' or not? Why ask me that?

MEROLA
(shrugs, walks around a moment)

You know, this place could be cleaner. We got a lotta people comin'.

BOMPKEE

Everything was straightened up last night.

MEROLA

That doesn't mean it's clean. That means it's neat.

BOMPKEE

Is this a suggestion?

MEROLA

It hasn't been swept up behind the bar. That's all. Not underfoot.

BOMPKEE

What's "not underfoot"?

MEROLA

It's crunchy. When you walk back there it's crunchy.

BOMPKEE

Maybe it's your shoes.

MEROLA

It's not my shoes.

BOMPKEE

New shoes change things.

MEROLA

It's got nothing to do with my shoes. Leather soles, yes, maybe, vibrafoam no. The place hasn't been properly swept.

BOMPKEE

Perhaps it was an oversight.

MEROLA

One day, unannounced, we get a new inspector in here, somebody young and possibly incorruptible. We could be in deep shit.

BOMPKEE
(marching to a closet)
Could I introduce you to Mr. Broom?
(pulls it out)

MEROLA
We might wanna re-evaluate the closing-up procedures, that's all I'm suggesting.

BOMPKEE
(broom in hand)
Oh? And maybe you'd like to switch assignments too while we're at it? I'll take over the books, pay all the bills.

MEROLA
Did I say that?

BOMPKEE
You can make vast improvements in operations. Use your financial expertise.

MEROLA
I was making a simple observation.

BOMPKEE
It didn't come out that way.

MEROLA
Whoever cleaned up last night was somewhat negligent.

           BOMPKEE
           (pause)
I wonder if it was because Rocky and I closed up alone since Donna asked to leave early. Donna had somewhere to go at three a.m. Yet again. And since Donna has let it be known around here that Donna sucks the occasional dick of one of the partners, I didn't wanna keep him waiting!

           MEROLA
Are we getting personal?

           BOMPKEE
     (approaching with the broom)
If you wanna criticize the way the place is run, stop knockin' off the help!

           MEROLA
       (moving towards him)
Who I associate with is none of your fuckin' business.

           BOMPKEE
The hell it's not!

> *He shoves the broom at Merola, who grabs it. Suddenly they are into a four-handed broom-wrestle. Bompkee forces him backwards, finally pinning Merola against the wall, the broom across his chest.*
>
> *Enter BOTTS in a camel hair overcoat. He looks at them struggling, goes to the bar, fixes himself a drink. They stop struggling, slowly lower the broom.*

                    BOTTS

You stopped dancin'?

                    BOMPKEE

Whoa, Ritchie—the paper!

                    BOTTS

I saw it.

                    MEROLA

You believe this?

                    BOTTS

I saw it. I had a late danish with Signor Caravelli.

                    BOMPKEE

Caravelli? Sunday?

                    BOTTS

He calls, I go.
                    (pause)
He won't be comin' to the party.

                    BOMPKEE

How come?

        Botts says nothing, waits.

                    MEROLA

I think I know what this is. It's not a problem.

                    BOTTS
Oh?

                    MEROLA
The note.

                    BOTTS
The note?

                    MEROLA
The bookkeeping was in arrears.

                    BOMPKEE
Meaning what?

                    MEROLA
It's been adjusted.
                    (pause)

                    BOTTS
He didn't make the payment.

                    BOMPKEE
He *what?*

                    MEROLA
There's no problem. Okay?

                    BOMPKEE
It was due Wednesday. We got this celebration—

MEROLA

I called the man, all right?

BOTTS

He said.

BOMPKEE

It's your assignment to handle finances. On time.

MEROLA

I know my job!

BOMPKEE

We got friends arrivin' in forty minutes to congratulate us on what you didn't do yet? This puts us in danger of being assholes.

MEROLA

It's no problem!

BOMPKEE

And you're gettin' on my case for crunchy floors?

BOTTS

Since there's no problem, why do you suppose Caravelli asks to see me?

MEROLA

I have no idea. Maybe he was lonely.

BOTTS

Does he call me in for *fun*? Talk sports? *Pussy*?

MEROLA
He gets his money, plus interest. Tomorrow.

BOTTS
(pause)
You told him Friday.

MEROLA
I got caught up.

BOMPKEE
"Caught up"? This is our balloon. We owe the man fifteen big, and you got "caught up"? I don't get it. Was it something serious? An operation? Did you have your balls removed??

MEROLA
You don't have to get it! It's an under-control situation.

BOTTS
He said you remind him of a used scumbag stuck to the floor of the men's room in Penn Station.

MEROLA
Which is where his mother works, you can tell him for me.

Botts lunges, grabs him by the collar, boosts him up.

BOTTS
Everything we got, everything we worked for is tied up here, with *Caravelli*! No bank touches us, remember? We were desperate to find this man!

MEROLA

Lemme go, Ritchie—

BOMPKEE

Make sure he gets the point.

BOTTS

You fuck with him, you fuck with us.

MEROLA

Okay!

Botts releases him. Fixing his clothes:

I said I'd straighten it out!

BOMPKEE

I wanna know why this happens at all.

MEROLA

I forgot!

BOMPKEE

We been leadin' up to this for how long? preparations, and you forgot?

MEROLA

Right. A distraction, pure and simple. I got caught up.

BOMPKEE

Are you somehow overworked?

BOTTS

You remove your fingers from whatever dark pie they've been stuck in all week and you deliver tomorrow.

BOMPKEE

By hand.

BOTTS

You become a servile, slithering creature. You rub his piss deep into your scalp and then you comb your hair down the middle. You kiss the walls of his decaying ass until he smiles! Am I making a point here? You think this is casual?
(turns his back)
I was sweating like a goddam pig. You know what it's like to sweat standin' still?
(pause)
Some fuckin' place he's got. Everything's suede. Suede couch. Suede chairs. Suede desk. I never saw a suede desk in my life. Who has a suede desk? He must've slaughtered an entire family of cows to furnish his apartment.
(pause)
He treated me with respect. He still believes in us. That's the point. We don't squander his support, faith, he stands by us.
(pause)
You could drive a cement truck through the living room. The living room alone is larger than the house of my dreams. With a television you could fuck on.
(shakes his head)
And we are his proteges. A guy like this picks up somebody to aid and abet he can't stand to be let down. It *reflects*. He loses face in his world. The other guys with suede desks think he's a jerk-off.

His admiration plunges. In his position it's total ego. Tarnish the man's ego, he turns nasty.

                    BOMPKEE
You had to tell him another war story?

                    BOTTS
I made one up on the way over. He knows we're vets; he's convinced we saw constant action. Every day, bang bang bang. He eats that up.
                    (pause)
He showed me his library. Not one book. All videotapes. He's got a copy of every war movie they ever made from *Green Berets* to *Casualties of War*. He's on his third copy of *Deerhunter*.
                    (shakes his head)
This is an actual combat groupie. You should see his rifles. Unbelievable. One room, all rifles. The history of rifles.

                    BOMPKEE
World War Two stuff? Any World Two weapons?

                    BOTTS
What?

                    BOMPKEE
M16s? Mausers?

                    BOTTS
How the fuck should I know?
                    (to Merola)
I told him you were one of those guys.

MEROLA

What guys?

BOTTS

From *Deerhunter*. In the cages with the rats, the Russian roulette. You escaped. That's your problem.

MEROLA

I escaped?

BOTTS

You meet him you tell him all about it. He loves the fact we were over there. Embroider. It was an ambush, you got separated from your patrol. It was foggy. They grabbed you. You shit your pants.
(A pause.)
It's why you fucked up. It's a memory thing. Every once in a while something happens, a sudden noise, a sound, a *click*, triggers a *mental lapse*, and you forget your responsibilities. It's *sad*.

BOMPKEE

Maybe you should see the movie again. Meryl Streep was still young.

MEROLA

The guy's a creep.

BOTTS

He is a fact of life.
(pause)
Starting Wednesday first of the month, we switch assignments. I do the books. You take over general maintenance.

MEROLA
Whoa! I fuck up one time—

BOTTS
Do I hear a second?

BOMPKEE
Second.

BOTTS
All in favor?

BOTTS AND BOMPKEE
Aye.

BOTTS
Opposed? *Opposed*?

MEROLA
Nay!

BOTTS
The motion carries. Let's put this behind us and have a drink. We got friends comin'!

He walks behind the bar to grab a bottle and glasses.

What's on the floor back here? It sticks.

Brings the bottle and the glasses downstage to the table.

So how'd we do last night?

                BOMPKEE
Good. Not too bad. We did okay.

                BOTTS
We did okay? As in "only okay"?

                BOMPKEE
Two-seventy-five in the register.

                BOTTS
For a Saturday night?

                BOMPKEE
It rained.

                BOTTS
This was a drizzle, a mist. Rain is something with puddles. Every Saturday night reads like shit—

                MEROLA
It's been an off month.

                BOTTS
You had your eyes on Rocky?

                BOMPKEE
He skimmed about ten bucks. Where were you?

BOTTS

I couldn't make it.

BOMPKEE

Oh?

BOTTS

And?

BOMPKEE

He drops in for twenty minutes. You don't show. Who the fuck is makin' all the cookies around here?

BOTTS
(To Merola.)
You told me you'd cover all night.

MEROLA

I stopped in. Somethin' came up.

BOTTS

Oh? How many times did it come up?

BOMPKEE

Weekends everybody's here! That's the deal—

BOTTS

All right.

BOMPKEE

I don't need silent partners!

                    BOTTS
Fuck you, I apologize. It won't get in the way again. My word.
                    (pause)
I'm havin' some problems.
                    (pause)

                    MEROLA
Problems?
                    (pause)
Maureen?

                    BOTTS
                (pouring the drinks)
Could be.

                    BOMPKEE
Serious?

                    BOTTS
Not necessarily.

                    BOMPKEE
A fight?

                    BOTTS
                (looks at him)
A spat.
                (raises his glass)
Cheers.

                    BOMPKEE AND MEROLA
Cheers.

> *They take a hit.*

                         BOTTS
I'll never talk to her again as long as I live.

> *He drinks down his shot. They look at each other as he pours another.*

                        BOMPKEE
This is a spat?

                         BOTTS
Call it what you will.

                        MEROLA
Are you postponing?

                         BOTTS
I think that's safe to say.

> *(pause)*

                        MEROLA
Was there a specific?

                         BOTTS
What "a specific"?

MEROLA

She lied, she stole, she cheated, she mouthed off? Like that.

BOTTS

None of the above.

BOMPKEE

Bad breath? Body odor?

Merola looks at him, so does Botts.

Oh, you think that's insignificant? Personal details are highly significant at the start of a relationship. You don't like the way someone smells do you marry them? Are you nuts? That's number *one*, believe it or not. It's *natural*. Animals do it.

MEROLA

You walk around sniffing every girl you meet?

BOMPKEE

I suppose you think the perfume industry is a joke? Billions of dollars every year, researched, advertised, devoted to what? Smell. Is that by chance? They *know* something: you can trick people into love. Guys will swoon from perfume, convinced they are madly in love. Then, later, you catch a whiff of the broad when she's forgotten to apply her stuff. Who is *this*? She doesn't smell good at all. I want my mother! I have fallen in love with a bottle of scent. It becomes an *unconscious* pattern. More than one poor bastard realizes too late in life that every single girl he has ever dropped to his knees for—used Replique.

They're looking at him.

BOTTS

It's not smell-related.

MEROLA

Maybe you don't wanna talk about it.

Silence.

BOTTS
(quietly)

What is it about women?

MEROLA

An alien culture.

BOTTS

But we need them.
(pause)
The right one. A deep breath.
(shakes his head)
It shouldn't be so tough. It should be easy. I like you, you like me, let's like each other.
(pause)
The language doesn't work out. It stops functioning. Somethin'—

MEROLA

We're from entirely different hemispheres. When they get serious, we get terrified. We get serious, they become victorious and cut off our balls.

(pause)

Nothing long-term lasts.

BOTTS

Mary.

MEROLA

Mary.

They toast Mary, Bompkee doesn't join in.

BOMPKEE

I'm under restraint.

They look at him.

As of yesterday. A court order.

BOTTS

For what?

BOMPKEE

I gotta stay away from the house.

BOTTS

From Mary?

MEROLA

For what reason?

BOMPKEE
(hesitates)
She says I threaten her. And the kid. She's frightened.

BOTTS
You?

BOMPKEE
She says.

MEROLA
How?

BOMPKEE
I holler at 'em. I scare 'em. I'm told.

BOTTS
And this is true?

BOMPKEE
I don't know.

MEROLA
What does that mean?

BOMPKEE
I have these moments. It's not clear. Usually after a few beers. Somethin' gets me angry—
(shrugs)
Then I fall asleep. I wake up accused.

BOTTS
How long's this been goin' on?

BOMPKEE
What she says? Years.

MEROLA
Can she verify this?

Bompkee shrugs.

BOTTS
She's got a lawyer?

BOMPKEE
(nods)
A woman.

They react with dismay.

BOTTS
What are the chances this actually happens?

BOMPKEE
I look at her. I hear what she's sayin'. I see my kid—
(pause)
I feel like somebody's been in my house terrifyin' my family. Turns out it's me!

A silence.

BOTTS
Hey. We'll do somethin'.

MEROLA
There's places we can go. Groups. Organizations. Self-help. Maybe the VA. Like that.

BOTTS
I'll talk to Mary first thing. She comin' over here for this?

Bompkee shakes his head No.

She's always been reasonable with me. We'll talk.

MEROLA
We work together.

BOTTS
Go through this.

BOMPKEE
Right—

BOTTS
If necessary we hire an attorney, protect your rights.

MEROLA
There's plenty of lawyers. Under every rock.

BOTTS
We look for one who's tough, maybe with ethics.

MEROLA

I can't believe she kicked him outta the house. This is turnin' out to be some day. That photo in the paper, you and Maureen, the skydiver—

BOTTS

The what?

MEROLA

Whoa!

BOMPKEE

You didn't hear about this—

MEROLA

On the way over were crossin' the street at Walnut and First, that new luxury building? I step off the curb, thump! splat! At our feet, in the gutter, arms out, face down, a guy!

BOTTS

This is true?

MEROLA
(grabs his coat)
All over the coat! What is this? Brain juice.

BOTTS

What'd you do?

BOMPKEE

We left.

MEROLA

The doorman comes out, takes a look, whips off his uniform, covers him up. Except the hands, stickin' out.

BOTTS

The new condo on Walnut and First? The Modigliani.

MEROLA

Exactly the one. An unbelievable moment in time. In a pin-stripe suit. Shoes with tassels. On a Sunday.

BOMPKEE

Tell him about the rings.

MEROLA

The rings! There's a goddam ring on this guy's pinkie, a star sapphire, size of an egg.

BOTTS

What?

BOMPKEE

(throws his arms out, drops his head into a spread-eagle)
His hand!

MEROLA

Right next to it, the adjacent finger, diamonds. A cluster. This is on one hand! Two baseballs.

BOMPKEE

A flying jewelry store—

BOTTS
(takes this in)
Pin-stripe suit?

MEROLA
(nods)
The hand is stickin' out from under the doorman's coat. Both stones, intact. If he lands the other way, hand down—smithereens, a total loss.

BOTTS
Star-sapphire, diamond cluster, pin-stripe suit?

They look at him.

I saw this guy.
(pause)
He was leavin' Caravelli's apartment.

A silence.

BOMPKEE
Sonofabitch.

MEROLA
You're sure?

BOTTS
How many rings like that in this city? This state. One hand? I step in, he leaves, escorted by Lurch and Sluggo.

They stare at each other, stunned.

                     BOMPKEE
             (makes a pushing motion)
Caravelli's army.
                         (pause)

                      MEROLA
                     (to Botts)
I think you're a material witness.

                     BOMPKEE
Possibly a suspect.

                      MEROLA
Possibly in big demand.

                       BOTTS
                       (calm)
Okay. Caravelli knows I won't finger him, but maybe I vanish for a while.
                  (to Merola)
Tomorrow early, you take Caravelli his money. Daybreak.

                     BOMPKEE
Lock it in.

                       BOTTS
No distractions.
                       (pause)
Where can I go it won't cost a fortune?

BOMPKEE
Your cousin down the shore?

BOTTS
His kids drive me nuts—their noses run all the time. They smell like piss.

A silence.

MEROLA
(struggling)
It can't be done.

BOMPKEE
What can't be done?

MEROLA
The balloon.

BOTTS
Meaning what?

MEROLA
There are no current funds available.

BOMPKEE
Whatta you talkin' about? We're okay. We still got the cash.

MEROLA
We are not liquid.

BOTTS

What "liquid"? Did you pay Caravelli or not?

MEROLA

No. He was not paid what we owed him.

BOMPKEE

So?

BOTTS

And?

A pause.

MEROLA

The cash was invested.

(long pause)

BOTTS

Go over this with great care, Rickey.

BOMPKEE

What exactly are you suggesting?

BOTTS

Be very precise.

BOMPKEE

You invested our money?

MEROLA
I saw an opportunity to move us into a strong position and I took it.

BOTTS
You moved us into a "strong position"?

BOMPKEE
Our money? You gambled it?

MEROLA
A chance to triple our reserves. Fast.

BOMPKEE
What "reserves"? That's all we got!

BOTTS
How much of our cash did you move into this strong position?

MEROLA
Every penny.
(silence)

BOMPKEE
Exactly where is the money?

MEROLA
Commodities.

BOTTS
I'm listenin'.

MEROLA
Soybeans.

BOMPKEE
Soybeans.

MEROLA
Futures. On good advice. Gasahol is coming back. It's a soybean by-product.

BOTTS
And?

MEROLA
They haven't performed as expected.

BOMPKEE
Who hasn't performed as expected?

MEROLA
(deep breath)
The bottom appears to have fallen out of the soybean market. As of Friday.

BOTTS
(long pause)
So whatta we have left?

MEROLA
(pause)
Nothin'.

A silence.

BOMPKEE
Suppose tomorrow soybeans go up? Through the roof.

MEROLA
It's too late.

BOMPKEE
It's too late?

BOTTS
(pause)
Can we pay Caravelli?

MEROLA
Whatever came in over the bar this weekend, that's it.

They take that in.

BOMPKEE
We can't even pay the bills?

MEROLA
Everything.

BOMPKEE
Everything.
(pause)
We've totally busted?

MEROLA
Right. I'm not hidin' anything. It hits, we pay him off, we still keep a bundle. We were on the verge of major capitalism! At our fingertips.

Botts swings and hits him in the gut. He doubles over.

BOTTS
Ten bucks in your pocket and you're a big fuckin' player.

Turns, picks up a chair and throws it, pushes over a table, rages around the room.

BOTTS
Every sales pitch you've ever heard, as long as the guy is wearin' a clean suit, you're in. Say "stockbroker" and you come in your pants. Who are these people? Dressed-up guys sellin' phony shit. You think if they believed in what they were doin' they'd buy it and then sell? No way. They're confidence men. Fancy assholes. One day this is suddenly good, the best, they say buy. Overnight somehow it turns to shit? Now they say sell. Does that inspire confidence? The country leans on this? A buncha guys makin' themselves millions, tellin' everybody it's what's good for America? Bullshit. It's good for them. Plunder the shit outta the country and say it's good for business. Go home laughin' and wipe their nose on the drapes!
(pause)
We spend, every week of our lives since the day we got back scramblin' up outta the fuckin' hole, crawl up outta the slime one fingernail at a time, finally seein' some daylight and you do what? You buy soybeans!

BOMPKEE
Jack and the fuckin' beanstalk.

BOTTS
There's guys flyin' out windows for less than this!

BOMPKEE
And we got thirty-five people comin' over to help celebrate it!
(a beat)
Maybe we could take out a loan. Pay him off.

BOTTS
A bank? No one's gonna touch us. Sonofabitch!

BOMPKEE
We still got the place, Ritchie. Maybe he'll give us an extension.

BOTTS
An extension? For how long? And where do we get the fifteen big should he grant us this "extension?" Which by then will be twenty big.
(pours a big hit from the bottle)
And the bills? The weekly nut? It vanishes? Along with the customers.
(looking down at Merola)
I'll kill him.

Botts makes a move towards Merola but Bompkee steps between them.

BOMPKEE

Hey, we drag the Arabs in by the nose! Next week? Arab week! One beer, free couscous. The whole month free couscous. It's dirt-cheap pasta shit. We give it away!

BOTTS

What the fuck are you talkin' about?

BOMPKEE

We reduce the nut.

BOTTS

We what?

BOMPKEE

Move back into operations. He waits tables. You tend bar, cook, whichever you want.

BOTTS

You don't seem to comprehend. It's beyond that. We are beyond deep shit.

BOMPKEE

No! We fire everybody. Rocky, Donna, the dishwashers. Assume control.

BOTTS

Of what? This is life and death.

BOMPKEE

You wanna give up? Everything we worked for?

BOTTS
It's gone. Face it. We're makin' travel plans.

BOMPKEE
Unh, unh. I don't do that. I'm not ready for that. We find a way.

BOTTS
The best we can hope for is lose the place.

BOMPKEE
No! No way. We do not lose this place!

A silence.

BOTTS
I wanna put my hands around his neck right now till his fuckin' eyeballs pop into my mouth.
 (pause)
Whatta you do when you wanna strangle people you're supposed to love?
 (pause)
A spat! I'd like to take her arm, pull it up behind her back and she's smilin' thinkin' it's a game. But its no game. I'd keep bendin' and she'd yell that first quick one, thinkin' I'd stop fast. But I wouldn't stop. I'd introduce her elbow to her neck, hear somethin' snap.
 (pause)
The only person I can count on is in a fuckin' nuthouse!

After a moment, Merola goes to the table with the glasses, braces himself and pours a shot.

MEROLA

We do some catering.

They look at him.

We go back to him. We *beg*. We lower ourselves. We grovel. *I* grovel. If he wants his money back he needs us. Workin', not stiff. He has no use for us deceased. So he makes us a deal. Some time.
(knocks back the shot)
We start with small parties. Intimate affairs. Celebrations. Wakes.
(nods, drinks)
There is no place in this entire area that will furnish a decent group meal.
(getting into it)
We work double time. Keep the bar goin' up front. We got the kitchen and the equipment, the know-how. So, long hours, a little advertising, a new angle. Presto, back in the ballgame.

Botts suddenly leaps at him but Bompkee steps between them, grabs Botts, holds him back.

MEROLA

What? What? It's a suggestion. I fucked up! Okay. I saw an opening and I went for it—

BOTTS

You asshole!

                MEROLA

Right. And suppose it *hits*, then what am I? It happens all the time! Guys get rich off commodities. It was there. The potential was there. We're set up for life.

                (pause)

I didn't steal. I gambled. I wanted to come through for us. The big time. Outta sight money. A whole new thing!

        Botts, calmer, disgusted, turns his back. Bompkee stays between them.

                MEROLA

I see it out there, within reach. What am I supposed to do, shut my eyes?

                BOTTS

Suppose you struck it rich in soybeans? Do we hear about it? Who's to say you don't pay off Caravelli and hook the stash, buy a Rolex?

                MEROLA

Don't say that, Ritchie.

                BOTTS

Who's to say?

                MEROLA

I don't do that!

                BOTTS

Oh? There's something you stop at?

BOMPKEE
He wouldn't do that, Ritchie.

BOTTS
You have that in writing?

BOMPKEE
We're buddies, for chrissake.

BOTTS
Is this what buddies do to each other? We don't come up with somethin' fast we're dead meat here!

MEROLA
Gimme a break, Ritchie—

BOTTS
Do you feel like shit? Is hot, strained shit runnin' through your veins? You feel like your mouth is full of somebody's old jock? Accept it. Live it. For as long as you got left.

MEROLA
Okay! I lost some self-control. Jeezus.
    (pause)
Be forgiving, will you please.
    (pause)
I screwed my buddies.
    (pause)
I been goin' nuts!

Silence. Botts turns away, leaning on the bar. Merola puts his head in his hands. Bompkee picks up the table, straightens the chairs.

BOMPKEE

This could be one of the great all-time parties.
(pause)
Ritchie, get the crackers and the dip. I'll heat up the wings.

He looks down at Merola, walks over to the broom, grabs it, walks back. He leans the broom against Merola.

BOMPKEE

You better sweep behind the bar. There's a whole lotta crunchy shit back there.

Botts exits into the kitchen. Bompkee goes to the bar. Merola finally gets it together and rises with the broom in his hand. The LIGHTS drop.

END ACT ONE

ACT TWO

The lights rise on a warehouse. There are three old wooden chairs. On the floor is a sleeping pallet, too thin to be called a mattress. There will be moments when this will seem like a room, or a shelter, a place in the world, or the loss of it.

Botts, Bompkee, and Merola explode into the dark room wearing identical black masks and black raincoats, out of breath, cursing.

Merola climbs a ladder and, with Bott's help, hooks a cable up to a light fixture, cursing as he works.

Bompkee carries a space heater. He goes to a window, starts to look out.

BOTTS

Get away from there.

BOMPKEE

The window—

BOTTS

Don't I know that? Don't I know what that is?

MEROLA

Sonofabitch—sonofabitch! A goddam blizzard!

BOTTS

Good shit! Do you believe it? Do you believe *this*? Who are we? Who the fuck can we *be*?

BOMPKEE

Maybe we shouldda parked around the corner.

BOTTS

Corner? What *corner*? There are no corners here. There is no corner.

BOMPKEE

Somewhere else then. Just *somewhere else.*

MEROLA

He's right. The car's down there and we're up here. There's a connection.

BOMPKEE

There's no cars, there's no corners, no sidewalks, no pavement, no buildings—

BOTTS

It's an abandoned area!

BOMPKEE

Just a goddam red Cadillac Seville in the middle of fuckin' Dresden.

BOTTS
(looks at him)
Don't start in on World War Two again. That's all I'm gonna say. We got enough problems here.

BOMPKEE
It's conspicuous!

BOTTS
No. No, this is the last place anybody is gonna look for a Cadillac Seville, you shithead.

MEROLA
Yeah. And it's the first place they're gonna find it when they're not lookin'.

The light comes on. They take the place in. Remove the masks.

BOMPKEE
Why didn't we think about this? Why didn't we think about the goddam car?

BOTTS
Because we had a fuck-up. And when you have a fuck-up it throws things off. Things go askew. That's what happened here, unless I'm mistaken. Unless I'm totally out of my mind. Unless you've got a better explanation!

He raises a chair off the ground, slams it down and it shatters. They look at it. A pause—

BOMPKEE
All right. Where the hell are we?

BOTTS
The Bronx. What's it look like, Bermuda?

BOMPKEE
I don't mean *where* are we. I mean where *are* we?

MEROLA
Why did we come here? We didn't discuss this.

BOTTS
Where the hell else would we have gone without more driving? This was the original plan.

BOMPKEE
We shouldda got out and walked away.

BOTTS
(stares at him)
You know, if I hadn't finished all your homework I'd have no idea how stupid you really are.

BOMPKEE
A big help you were.
(to Merola)
Professor Borts.

BOTTS
We're in deep shit!

(a beat)
I told Caravelli we were onto somethin' solid. We'd have it all before the end of his goddam "arrangement."

                BOMPKEE
Hey, we still got four weeks. He knows we're tryin'.

                BOTTS
"Trying"? Trying doesn't mean shit in the business world. Success is what counts. This was our shot, goddammit! Tendin' bar, waitin' tables in our own place? While he empties the register every night!

                MEROLA
So we explain. We ran into some bad luck. Like that.

                BOMPKEE
At least it's still ours, we still got the place—

                BOTTS
He's got us. We're indentured assholes. Every day, every week the debt augments and we're makin' tips!

                BOMPKEE
He couldda broke our legs, Ritchie.

                BOTTS
(looks at him)
It's always an option.

      A silence.

BOMPKEE
Mary'll never believe me. Every step I take I'm walkin' on eggs.

MEROLA
Relax. She loves you. That's why she let you back in.

BOTTS
She doesn't need to know. It hasn't got that far—we're gettin outta this.
(pause)
How the fuck did this happen?

BOMPKEE
You asked who she's been tempin' for lately, that's how.

MEROLA
(Disgusted.)
Another fuckin' dentist.

BOMPKEE
Doctor Nushkin.

MEROLA
Nushkin's gold!

BOTTS
I mean *this*. Not that. I know that. I asked her, she told me. A receptionist.

MEROLA
He had a lotta balls for a dentist. I'll tell you that.

BOMPKEE
Most dentists, if they had any balls they woudda been doctors.
> *(pause)*

MEROLA
Nushkin. I wish I never heard the name.
> *(pause)*

BOMPKEE
How did we invent such a stupid idea? What were we thinkin'?

MEROLA
It looked good on paper.

BOTTS
It was a commendable plan! We caught the bus, we grabbed the dentist, we left the note, we took the car, we hit the thruway, we came across the Tappan Zee, down the Deegan to the tollbooth.
> *(pause)*

It was well-executed up to a point. You cannot anticipate the unknown.

BOMPKEE
(to Merola)

You were right next to him.

MEROLA
Oh. We're gonna go into *that*? You wanna go into that? I'll go into that if you want. If you want to go into that, go ahead. Go into it. I'm waitin'. I'm here. Let's go into it. The whole thing is my fault! Right? You wanna bring that up again? Go ahead.

                    BOTTS

You were right there.

                    MEROLA

And you had no change!

                    BOTTS

Nobody had change.

                    BOMPKEE

You don't drive up to the exact-change without the exact change. A two-year-old can tell you that, a fucking *infant*.

                    MEROLA

We assumed you had had it. We gave you the benefit of the fucking doubt, like always.

                    BOTTS

What's that mean, "like always"? What?

                    MEROLA

You name it, you got it.

                    BOMPKEE

You couldda drove straight to a guy. No one told you to go to exact-change.

                    BOTTS

Brilliant. I drive up to a guy, roll down the fucking window, hand him a buck and Nushkin screams, "Help, I'm being kidnapped!"

MEROLA

I wouldda blown him away.

BOTTS

With what? You had no gun, shithead.

MEROLA

Nushkin doesn't know that! What's he think I got stickin' through my raincoat, my dick?

BOMPKEE

Sure. How's Nushkin supposed to know his dick is only an inch long? You don't even need a license for that.

BOTTS

You can't get a license for that.

BOMPKEE

Most states you gotta throw it back.

MEROLA

Funny I'm the one who manages to get laid around here. Why is that?

BOTTS

You ever ball somebody you were proud of? Introduce around in daylight?

MEROLA

Right. Only I didn't ask the fuckin' dentist for forty cents to go down the Major Deegan Expressway so he could be kidnapped!

BOMPKEE
No, but you let him drop the change on the front seat, open the goddamn door and run while we're pickin' it up!

MEROLA
And what am I supposed to do, tackle fuckin' Nushkin in front of five hundred vehicles and drag him back inside the car? How would that've looked: "Nothin' goin' on here folks, just a friendly little game of kidnap-the-dentist!"

BOTTS
You probably wouldda missed the tackle.

MEROLA
Oh. Joe fuckin' Montana.

After a moment.

BOTTS
I think we gotta stop harpin' on the past. We don't bring it up, any of it. Let it be. Go on from there. We got a lotta thinkin' to do.

He sits down. The chair crumbles under him. He falls to the floor and bounces up fast.

BOMPKEE
What about the car? Let's hone in on the fuckin' car.
(pause)

BOTTS
(the plan)
We leave the car where it is. When we leave here, we forget the car. There's no trace of us in the car.

BOMPKEE
Fingerprints.

MEROLA
We wore gloves, shithead. You forgot about that?

BOMPKEE
I removed my gloves.

BOTTS
You removed your gloves.

BOMPKEE
My hands were sweating.

MEROLA
His hands were sweating.

BOMPKEE
They started to itch. The psoriasis—I forgot. I took 'em off. Fuck me.

MEROLA
No wonder he's worried about the car.

                        BOMPKEE
My prints are on file.

                        MEROLA
Everybody who *went's* on file, enlisted, drafted—

                        BOTTS
You take a rag, you go outside, you wipe the interior of the car. Wherever you touched!

                        BOMPKEE
Who's got a rag?

                        MEROLA
Use a sock.

                        BOTTS
Did you remember your socks? Take one off Pretend it's a rag. Be thorough.

                        BOMPKEE
Where's the keys?

                        BOTTS
In the ignition where they're supposed to be. You don't need the keys to wipe the car—can you handle this or should we call in a cleaning service?

   Bompkee exits. Silence.

MEROLA

He removed his gloves.

BOTTS

Another fuckin' learning experience.
    (looks out the window)
He does nothing the way you expect him to. You ever notice that?

A silence.

MEROLA
(watches him)

So, how's your sister?

BOTTS
(looks up, amazed)

My sister?

MEROLA

I don't see much of her.

BOTTS
(looks at him)

Why are you askin' me about my sister?

MEROLA

I was wonderin'—she seein' anybody?

BOTTS

Jeannie? She's seein' somebody.

                        (pause)
A mystery man.

                        MEROLA
How do you know?

                        BOTTS
I don't know. I baby-sit. She goes out.
                        (pause)
I think he's married. What is this about?

                        MEROLA
She was beautiful in high school, with that braid, her complexion—
                        (pause)
I always liked your sister.

   Botts is looking at him hard.

She's down to earth. No bullshit.
                        (pause)
Send her my love.

   Botts is still staring at him. Merola turns, looks around.

                        MEROLA
This isn't much of a place.

                        BOTTS
That's why it's abandoned. If it was a decent place, if it had character and charm and heat—you'd find tenants. There'd be *people*

here. It would be occupied. It wouldn't have served our purpose. It was an ideal situation.

      (pause)

Nushkin sits there. That box conceals him from the window. The window commands the exterior.

      (pause)

It's perfect for what we had in mind.

      MEROLA

You raised your mask.

      BOTTS

What?

      MEROLA

When you were lookin' for change, you raised your mask.

      BOTTS

So what? I couldn't see down. You ever tried to see down with a mask on?

      MEROLA

He saw your face. Nushkin.

      BOTTS

What are you talkin' about? He was behind me.

      MEROLA

Your profile. He saw your profile.

(pause)

BOTTS
What's on your mind, Ricky? You got somethin' on your mind?

MEROLA
Dentists remember things.

BOTTS
He didn't see my teeth, did he? He saw half a face and no teeth. What's goin' on here? He removes his gloves, I show my face, Ricky looks good? Is that it?
(pause)
And you're still seein' Mary, right? See her in high school that makes her yours? She's his *wife*, remember?

MEROLA
She calls.

BOTTS
Don't tell me that. You mean *you* call! That's some code of ethics you got. He married her, didn't he? Accept it. And you married Edith. That was *fate*.

Merola shrugs.

You're a class guy, Ricky. He's your buddy, for chrissake. Remind me never to introduce you to anyone with tits.

MEROLA
He's seein' your sister.

BOTTS

He's *who*?

They hear a noise, and jump at the sound. Bompkee returns.

BOMPKEE
(*entering*)

The keys are in the ignition.

BOTTS

That's what I told *you*. You didn't have to come back up here to tell me that. That's *insignificant*, you shithead.

BOMPKEE

And the doors are locked.

BOTTS

Locked?

BOMPKEE

From within.

BOTTS

The doors are locked from within?

MEROLA

You musta locked your door.

BOTTS
I musta locked my door? You musta locked yours, he musta locked his, if they're all locked.

MEROLA
I didn't lock mine. I consciously didn't lock my door.

BOMPKEE
I never lock a door.

BOTTS
Am I an asshole? Did I walk around locking four doors? In the snow? Funny, I have no recollection of doing that.
(pause)

MEROLA
It's got a device.

BOTTS
It's what?

MEROLA
A device. A power lock. The driver locks his door, they all lock. The driver opens his door, they all open. The driver puts up the windows. The driver puts down the windows. The driver opens the trunk. The driver locks the trunk. The driver releases the hood, the driver secures the hood. The driver flips on the interior lights. The driver flips off the interior lights. The driver is in total fucking *command*! He rules the car. It's an entire Nazi operation. A master-control device. They got it from the Germans. Detroit

imported it from the fuckin' Nazis. Mercedes had it first. Hitler used it in his limousine. It was Hitler's device.

BOMPKEE

Hitler didn't drive.

MEROLA

What are you talkin' about?

BOMPKEE

Hitler didn't drive. He sat in the back.

MEROLA

How the fuck do you know where Hitler sat?

BOMPKEE

He was a *dictator*. Dictators don't drive. They get driven.

MEROLA

So what?

BOMPKEE

He would never have given all that control to his driver.

MEROLA

He shouldna locked the door, that's the bottom line.

BOTTS

If you knew so much about this device why didn't you tell me before I locked all the doors?

MEROLA
I didn't know it then. I *deduced* it.

BOTTS
It was an unconscious act.

MEROLA
Who was supposed to research everything regarding wheels? Inside and out? Who, me?

BOTTS
I didn't know it had a "power lock"!

MEROLA
It was your assignment.

(pause)

BOMPKEE
He probably had the control panel built into the back seat. That's what he would've done upon assuming power.

They look at him.

BOTTS
Attempted kidnapping, grand larceny and you're talkin' about Adolph Fucking Hitler. Your fingerprints are out there!

MEROLA
We'll have to break in.

BOTTS
We'll have to break in.

(pause)

BOMPKEE
If they catch you breakin' into a car you already stole, what is that—*attempted* robbery, or robbery?

BOTTS
We got no tools. You can't get into these cars without equipment.

MEROLA
Bricks.

BOTTS
Bricks?

BOMPKEE
We smash a window—we're in.

BOTTS
No shit. I'm thinkin' it through. We smash a window, open the door, remove the prints—leave the premises.

BOMPKEE
Come on, let's do it.

They start to go.

                        MEROLA

Hold it.

They stop.

A lotta those cars with command panels? There's a mandatory alarm system. You lock the doors, you engage the alarm.

                        BOTTS

It's loud?

                        MEROLA

A piercing wail from two miles off.

                        BOMPKEE

Compulsory.

                        BOTTS

What?

                        BOMPKEE

Mandatory means you got a choice. Compulsory, you got no choice. It's a compulsory alarm system, it comes with the vehicle.

                        BOTTS

We can't break in.

                        BOMPKEE

Some of 'em are hooked right into the police station. You break in, the alarm goes off, the police are notified electronically. That part is mandatory—notifying the police. With that option you have a choice. It's a mandatory option. My cousin works for Chrysler—

                    MEROLA

Who, Jerry?

                    BOMPKEE

Vince.

                    MEROLA

Vince? You told me Vince was laid off.

                    BOMPKEE

He was laid off. That don't mean he forgot. Just 'cause you get laid off you don't hand in your brains.

                    MEROLA

When'd he get laid off?

                    BOMPKEE

About a month ago. They caught him walkin' out with a couple tape decks.

                    MEROLA

Tape decks? That's not laid off, that's canned. That's fired. You don't get laid off for theft.

                    BOMPKEE

Not technically.

MEROLA

What's "not technically"?

BOMPKEE

He wasn't outside the factory. They stopped him at the door—within.

MEROLA

Then what?

BOMPKEE

They accused him.

MEROLA

And?

BOMPKEE

He quit.

MEROLA

He quit.

BOMPKEE

That's right. He told 'em he'd been workin' at Chrysler seven and a half months. If he couldn't walk up to the door with a couple a tape decks under his arm, just walk up to the door—he didn't wanna work there anymore. So he quit. He doesn't like being accused. He's got a lotta pride.

MEROLA

First you say he works at Chrysler. Then he's laid off. Then he's fired. Now he quits—

BOMPKEE

Exactly. His status remains unclear. He's takin' a leave of absence.

MEROLA

A leave of absence? Let me ask you this—is the man behind bars?

BOMPKEE

What are you crazy? He's my cousin. He's home—for now.

BOTTS

We gotta trash the car.
                    (turns to them)
We gotta trash the car.

BOMPKEE

It's a Cadillac.

BOTTS

I see no alternative.
                    (pause)

BOMPKEE

How?

BOTTS

How? Gasoline.

MEROLA

Where's the gasoline?

BOTTS

We buy it. There's a Gulf station, it's not far.

BOMPKEE

It's a diesel engine.

BOTTS

So what?

BOMPKEE

Diesel doesn't ignite like gasoline. It's stationary.

BOTTS

We don't buy diesel, you asshole, we buy gas. We're not interested in driving the fuckin' car, we're gonna blow it up.

MEROLA

They won't sell you gas without a car. It's the law.

BOTTS
(the plan)

We ran outta gas. We're willin' to leave a sizable deposit on a can, two, three times its value, insuring our return. They never say no. If you don't show up they pocket the cash. They're small-timers, gas station attendants.

MEROLA

They'll wanna send a truck. That's how they make their dough—send a truck, charge some cocksucker ninety bucks. And they hit you for the gas.

BOMPKEE

Ninety bucks? We get on our feet again maybe we should expand into the garage business. Everybody we knows got a car. We could open a garage.

MEROLA

You wanna open a garage?

BOTTS
(slow boil)

Do you see Nushkin? Is Nushkin here? The fifty grand, where is it? Is it on its way? Are we meeting Mrs. Nushkin on the Cross Bronx Expressway with the gold fillings and the cash? Are we ready to pay off the Man? Is everything going as *planned*?
(pause)
We are hung out to dry, remember? We're workin' for tips. Our nuts are in a vise. Plus there is an angry, fucking dentist running along the Major Deegan Expressway at this moment, screamin' for help. His car is down there, *locked*, with your fingerprints on it. We just blew our first attempt at an organized crime and you're talkin' to us about opening a garage? Are you nuts? We could get sent away for this!

BOMPKEE

I withdraw the suggestion.

MEROLA

So we get the gas, then what?

BOTTS

We pour it over the entire car. We pour it under the car, especially near the trunk. We *douse* the car.

BOMPKEE

And?

BOTTS

And we ignite it. What do you wanna do, swim in it?

BOMPKEE

Who?

BOTTS

Who what?

BOMPKEE

Who ignites it?

BOTTS

Why do you ask?

BOMPKEE

It's a highly flammable substance. That's why I ask.

MEROLA

We'll do it in unison. How's that? All three of us. Poof!

                    BOMPKEE
With a match?

                    BOTTS
A match, a blowtorch, whatever's handy.

                    BOMPKEE
Ever since you quit smokin' we don't carry matches.
                    (pause)

                    BOTTS
We'll get the matches at the gas station.
                    (pause)

                    MEROLA
"Excuse me. I'd like a gallon of gasoline and a book of matches, please." I don't know—

                    BOTTS
You buy a pack of cigarettes. That's how you do it. Along with the gas. Then you remember the matches.

                    BOMPKEE
A regular book of matches? Were gonna bend down, strike a match, touch it to gasoline? It sounds foolish to me.

                    MEROLA
We'll make a torch.

                    BOMPKEE
Outta what?

BOTTS
Whatever's around! We'll find somethin'.

BOMPKEE
It's snowin' out there. It's sticking.

MEROLA
Socks! A sock. We tie it to a brick. Dip it in the gas. We light it from a distance, we throw the brick at the car. Poof!

BOMPKEE
You light the sock and then throw the brick?

MEROLA
Right.

BOMPKEE
Who holds the brick?

MEROLA
The sock is at one end!

BOMPKEE
It could go out when you throw it.

MEROLA
You ever light a sock?

BOMPKEE
No. I never lit a sock.

MEROLA

It's a version of the Molotov cocktail. They don't go out.

BOTTS

When did you ever light a sock?

MEROLA

I've seen it done. On television, all right? It works.

BOMPKEE

What show?

MEROLA

I don't recall. It was a show with violence.

BOMPKEE

And the sock didn't go out?

MEROLA

That's right. The sock didn't go out.

BOTTS

And they got a good head start too, is that right?

MEROLA

As I recall.

BOTTS

Who's got the best arm?

                    BOMPKEE
Baseball me. Football you.

                    BOTTS
This is a brick.

                    MEROLA
We'll do two. You can have a contest.

   Silence.

                    BOMPKEE
Who goes for the gas?

                    MEROLA
I'll get the gas.

                    BOMPKEE
You volunteer?

                    MEROLA
I'll get the gas.

                    BOTTS
How come?

                    MEROLA
                    (shrugs)
I feel like it.

BOMPKEE
You feel guilty?

MEROLA
Did I say that?

BOTTS
That's in the past. We're beyond guilt. Front seat, back seat, soybeans. It's over with.

BOMPKEE
Right. We're in this together. The whole way. And forget Nushkin. He's probably home washin' out his underwear by now.

MEROLA
Did you see the look on his face?

BOTTS
"Don't hurt me! Don't hurt me!"

They laugh.

BOMPKEE
I've always wanted to see a dentist in pain.
(pause)
How much for the gas can? Whatta you think?

BOTTS
Twenty bucks.
(to Merola)
Take thirty.

                    BOMPKEE
Here's ten.

                    MEROLA
It's a Gulf station?

                    BOTTS
A lotta lights. You walk north two blocks, you'll see the lights in the distance.

                    BOMPKEE
That's east.

                    BOTTS
              (with a look at Bompkee)
You'll see the lights. Get goin'.

                    BOMPKEE
Don't forget the matches!

Merola exits. Bompkee stands still, scratches his hand. A silence.

                    BOTTS
It's a fuckin' blizzard out there.

                    BOMPKEE
He'll make it. He's good in snow.

Botts looks at him, turns away.

I heard about this guy in Texas. San Antonio, Texas. He bought a snow plow. Everyone thought he was a jerk-off, including the salesman he bought it off. The average winter temperature in San Antonio, Texas is a hundred and eleven degrees and this guy buys a full-rig snow plow. The only one in the entire city.
(pause)
It snows.
(nods)
Two weeks after he buys it and they get a record thirteen inches snowfall. In Texas, A fucking blizzard.
(pause)
His life is solved!
(pause)
All you need is an idea and some luck.
(disgusted)
It snows here all the time.

BOTTS

So. You seein' my sister?

BOMPKEE
(surprised)

Your sister?

BOTTS

That's right. Are you seein' my sister?

BOMPKEE

Your sister's divorced.

BOTTS
Are you seeing her?

BOMPKEE
Jeannie?

BOTTS
That's her name, right.

BOMPKEE
Jeannie. No. No. I'm not seeing Jeannie. I have seen her, but I'm not seeing her.

BOTTS
When was the last time you saw her?

BOMPKEE
Not that long ago. Some time ago. I saw her a while ago.

BOTTS
A while ago? Am I mistaken or are you a married man? Did I recently negotiate with your wife to get you back in the house?

BOMPKEE
Who told you I was seein' Jeannie?

BOTTS
I heard.

BOMPKEE
From him?

BOTTS

I heard.

BOMPKEE

Did he tell you he's seein' Mary? Well he's not. My wife wouldn't see him, are you kiddin? But he tells you I'm seein' your sister to make him feel better about Mary not seein' him.
(pause)
Mary hasn't seen him since high school, since he started datin'—

BOTTS

Edith.

BOMPKEE

Edith. He poisons the atmosphere. But that's okay because Mary's not seein' him, so I don't give a shit.
(pause)
Who are you seein'?

BOTTS

Nobody special.
(pause)

BOMPKEE
(carefully)
So what happened with Maureen? You never said.

BOTTS

Maureen?

(considers)
Maureen opened Maureen's mouth about the one thing Maureen should never have opened Maureen's mouth *about*. She laughed. Thought it was funny I almost married someone ends up in an institution. *Laughed.*

BOMPKEE
You told Maureen about her?

BOTTS
It came up. I figured why not be frank.

BOMPKEE
You were up front.

BOTTS
Bitch! Laughs about an angel! It's done. Over. A concluded affair.

BOMPKEE
I guess there's no such thing as the perfect woman, you know? They all have flaws. Even the ones in the commercials have flaws. You can't *see* the flaws but they must be there—drivin' some guy in jeans and a T-shirt out of his fuckin' mind.

BOTTS
Maybe you should write a column.

BOMPKEE
(looks at him)
Mary said you were over the other night.

BOTTS
Mary said that?

BOMPKEE
She said.

BOTTS
I mightta dropped by. What night?

BOMPKEE
Sunday. League night.

BOTTS
I stopped by.

BOMPKEE
You saw Mary?

BOTTS
She was there.

BOMPKEE
The kid was asleep?

BOTTS
He wasn't visible. Maybe he was awake in bed.

Silence.

BOMPKEE
You watched some TV?

BOTTS

Whatever was on.

BOMPKEE

You knew it was league night?

BOTTS

I stopped in. I saw Mary. We *spoke*.

BOMPKEE

She said.

BOTTS

There was nothin' on.

BOMPKEE

You shoulda waited. We coulda had a beer. Somethin'.

BOTTS

I had a beer.

(pause)

So how'd you do?

BOMPKEE

Me? I won a case.

BOTTS

My sister's got league that night too.

BOMPKEE

Jeannie. I saw her.

BOTTS
You saw my sister?

BOMPKEE
Yeah. I saw her. She's lookin' good.

A pause.

BOTTS
So—you callin' him a liar?

BOMPKEE
Who?

BOTTS
Him.

BOMPKEE
(softly, not looking at him)
There's a lotta liars around.

Silence. Botts says nothing, stares at Bompkee.

BOTTS
(finally)
So. Nushkin. You think he's got anything to go on?

BOMPKEE
Nushkin?

BOTTS

Three guys with masks on, black raincoats and brown gloves wait for him outside his office, put him in his own car, say virtually nothing until they get to the toll booth and then he's gone? You tell me.

BOMPKEE

We're in good shape.

BOTTS

Except for the car.

BOMPKEE
(rubbing his hands)

The car. My fault.

BOTTS

The past is out of our hands. We go from here. You can't go forward mired in the past.
(pause)
Whatta you doin' for that rash?

BOMPKEE

Cream.

BOTTS

Cream?

BOMPKEE

It cost a fortune—a little tube of fuckin' cream. It's like a mortgage.

BOTTS

You always wanted a house.

BOMPKEE
(looks at him)

Yeah.

(silence)

You ever get tired, Ritchie?

BOTTS

Tired of what?

BOMPKEE

I don't know, livin' alone? Your mother upstairs, all these years.

BOTTS

I do okay. Some guys come back they walk out on their families. You think that's manly? Is that admirable? I don't do that. Say what you will. Who judges a man's behavior?

BOMPKEE
(after a moment)

I just wondered.

They look at each other.

I still have dreams. I dream a lot.

BOTTS

So.

BOMPKEE
I wouldn't wanna wake up alone in bed, that's all.

BOTTS
Like a dog?

BOMPKEE
What "a dog"?

BOTTS
Legs movin', kickin' out. Moan. Wake up fast, huffin', soaked with sweat. Like that. Well, fuck it.

A pause.

BOMPKEE
That night we went down to D.C. In the room. You didn't sleep so good.

BOTTS
What are you talkin' about?

BOMPKEE
I don't know what went on during the day. You two guys took off. I never saw you all day after breakfast.

BOTTS
We drank. First we did a little drinkin', then we drank.

BOMPKEE
So I heard. Maybe this was—unrelated to that.

BOTTS

Unrelated to what? Enter the language system, will you please.

BOMPKEE
(pause)

In your sleep. You were cryin'.

A pause.

BOTTS

I was?

BOMPKEE

You calmed down.

BOTTS

I did?

BOMPKEE

I patted you on the back a couple times.

BOTTS

You did?

Bompkee nods. Quietly:

It happens.

A pause.

BOMPKEE

Why you didn't come up there with me that day, look around. I'll never know.

BOTTS

We met these guys.

BOMPKEE

Just bein' there, the size of it.

BOTTS

I saw the thing.

BOMPKEE
(thinks)

I couldn't believe the size of it.
(pause)
Big. Mammoth. Granite. Just those slabs, you know, standin' there. Huge slabs. Black. Shiny. With the names. I got there I looked around. At first I'm thinkin' what the fuck is this? I mean just slabs, you know? I mean Lincoln and Jefferson are there, inside, actual statues. Then you start thinkin', well who are they gonna put? Who? Who could it be? There's nobody.
(shrugs)
And you start walkin' around. In front of you, behind you, on the side, over your head—all those names. You're surrounded by names. Fifty-eight thousand names, all etched onto the slabs. Every single, goddam name is there. Every one. Into the granite. Nineteen fifty-nine to nineteen seventy-five.

(pause)

At first you know, it's a little—you think, this is ridiculous, just names and slabs, slabs and names. I mean what the fuck is this! But I don't know, somethin' happens, it's like you can't leave. You can't stand it, but you stay.

(pause)

And it was quiet. There's all this raucous bullshit goin' on until you get up there, and then I mean nobody says hold it down or anything like that, just—it happens on your own. Like church. All these people, women, kids, old people holdin' hands, but nobody talks. It's spooky, you know? Everybody's huntin' for a name. Or if they found it then they just stand there, just stand there, say nothin' and stare at the letters. A long time. Tryin' to see somethin'—maybe a memory.

(pause)

You guys never showed up.

(pause, unnerved)

I was four feet away from where I was—I didn't move four feet! I was in a trance. It was like a goddam trance.

(shakes his head)

I had started to read all the names. I mean I went to nineteen fifty-nine. I began there. I tried to do that. Am I nuts? Is that weird?? I actually tried to do that and I could hardly get to sixty-three. Sixty-three! There's just too many names. You can't read fifty-eight thousand names. You can't! You can't do it. Just names? It can't be done! Just names?

(overcome)

All those names? Names and names and names and names and names and names—more names! All those names? Those guys! Just names?

Botts moves to him. The door suddenly opens and Merola returns, startling them.

MEROLA
(shaking off)
It's closed.

BOTTS
Closed? You went there? Was there a guy?

MEROLA
The lights were off. You think we could hook up this heater?

They look at him.

BOTTS
You didn't go all the way?

MEROLA
The lights were *off*. A gas station shuts off its lights, it's closed.

BOMPKEE
There mightta still been a guy there, closin' up.

BOTTS
He didn't go all the way. I'm in shock.

MEROLA
It was closed!

                    BOMPKEE
We're sittin' here freezing? waitin' for you?

                    MEROLA
And what am I, comfortable? You think it's *balmy* out there?

                    BOTTS
We send you on a mission, and this is the result?

                    MEROLA
It's a fuckin' blizzard out there.

                    BOTTS
You are a raging asshole!

                    MEROLA
The place was closed. *No lights.* No lights.

                    BOTTS
You check! You walk all the way up there. You drop to your knees. You beg the guy for a can of gas. You *beg*. You reach up, you suck his cock for a can of gas.

                    MEROLA
No, no. That's your specialty, you drop.

                    BOTTS
What?

           Botts moves towards Merola. Bompkee, from behind, grabs Botts.

BOMPKEE

Slow down. Slow down!

Botts pushes him out of the way, hard, starts after Merola again when Bompkee, angered, charges Botts from behind and knocks him down. Botts and Bompkee go at it on the floor, flailing and slugging.

MEROLA
(watching them, calmly)

Maybe it wouldda been fruitless. Once they shut off the lights they've already booked the pumps. That's it. The pumps are booked in. They wouldn't give gas to a raped nun once they book the pumps.

(moves to them)

Come on. Back off—back off!

He reaches to pull Botts off Bompkee. Botts turns and with a closed hand, slams his fist up into Merola's crotch. Merola doubles over, drops with a groan. They are all on the floor, in pain. After a long moment Botts rises, stumbles to a corner, sits.

Finally:

MEROLA

Okay. Okay. All right. All right. I'll go back there first thing. My responsibility.

BOTTS

Six, six-thirty a gas station usually opens up.

(pause)
There are guys we know, guys we knew, shitheads from high school. Guys no smarter than we are. You know their names. Today? Big successes. Money, cars, houses, homes, families—

MEROLA
Successful shitheads.

BOMPKEE
And we're scarin' dentists half to death.

BOTTS
These guys had nothin' goin'! You tell me.

MEROLA
Maybe havin' nothin' goin' in high school—don't mean what we thought.
(Beat.)
You know what's funny? I never figured I'd get this far with no kids. Holidays.

BOMPKEE
Hey, there's plenty of time for kids. You got your whole life ahead of you.
(a beat)
Most of it.
(a beat)
Half.
(pause)
The car's covered with snow.

MEROLA

The hood?

BOMPKEE

The hood, yeah.

Silence.

BOTTS

I go there. I visit her. The institution. You guys didn't know that. Every time, every visit there's always one moment, just, one. She looks right at me, she looks me in the eyes. Smiles.
(pause)
It's as if she's forgivin' me.
(a beat)
The only girl I can count on is in a fuckin' nuthouse and I put her there—

BOMPKEE

Hey, you didn't put her there, Ritchie. Don't say that.

BOTTS

Whatta you know?

MEROLA

The girl was sick.

BOTTS

No! She wouldda been just fine. The long run? Fragile. A fragile woman, fragile wife. So you handle that. Be gentle, read in bed, kid gloves, early nights. Tea. Simple devotion. Nothin's perfect.

Twenty-two-year-old me! Two days before the wedding and I force myself on an angel! I couldn't wait?
>(pause)

What's that long, two days?
>(a beat)

Marriage is forever.

>MEROLA
>(at the window)

Somebody's out there. Headlights!
>(headlights appear)

>BOTTS

Holy shit!

>*Botts jumps to unplug the light. They all hit the ground, scuttle across to the window.*

>BOMPKEE

Cops?

>BOTTS

Why do you ask me that? Aren't we lookin' out the same window?

>BOMPKEE

So who drives around a place like this ten miles an hour at night, circlin' around?

>*They watch.*

BOTTS
Okay, turn left—that's it . . .

BOMPKEE
Keep goin', goin' . . .

BOTTS
Outta here!

They exhale. Merola turns, hooks up the light.

MEROLA
(he's got it)
Car thieves.

They nod.

My guess? On the cell phone contactin' a chop shop. They cut a deal. Return, steal the vehicle, sell it for parts. Like that.

BOMPKEE
Why don't we do that?

BOTTS
We torch the fucking car! We got no choice. If they steal the car first, they take it off our hands. So much the better. We're okay till morning.
(pause)

MEROLA
We gotta start thinkin' beyond tomorrow morning—

Botts looks at him.

BOMPKEE

I told Mary we might go down the shore. Gamble. Just the three of us hangin' out. She tends not to believe me.

MEROLA

She'll believe you. They want to believe us. That's their total problem.

BOMPKEE
(pause)

This worked out, the extra cash, I was gonna get her a car. Nothin' fancy. Fix her up with a few lessons. I think I wouldda leased.
(pause)
She's draggin' the kid all over on buses, bad weather—goin' to work.
(Thinks.)
She told me one night she's standin' at her desk, cleanin' up. Nushkin gets down on his knees behind her, he puts his arms around her knees and he kisses the back of her legs. She jumps a mile. He begs her to let him kiss her all over. Begs. He's shakin'—his whole body. He starts to cry.
(pause)
She's tellin' me this. I'm thinkin', what's she doin' there? That's my wife.

BOTTS

Why didn't you tell us this?

MEROLA

Turns out the guy's a creep.

BOMPKEE
(suddenly realizes)

Holy shit.

(a beat)

She's gonna get questioned!

(panic)

He gets back, he calls the cops. The F.B.I.! They pull in everybody who works for him, the hygienist, the receptionist—she will get grilled! Fuck *me*.

BOTTS

Relax! She knows nothing. She has nothin' to conceal. They could give her a lie-detector, she passes brilliantly. She has been kept in the total dark. Right or wrong?

BOMPKEE

Okay. Right. That's right. But she still gets questioned.

BOTTS

And, and—forget the F.B.I.

BOMPKEE

They always come in on a kidnappin'.

BOTTS

What "always"? The victim is at large. A free man. Local authorities, at their *discretion*, invite *in* the F.B.I. Not automatic.

                    BOMPKEE
                    (a breath)
We got lucky.

                     BOTTS
My point.

                    MEROLA
                    (painful)
I said somethin'.

    They look at him.

To Mary. The other day. She wanted to know what we were up to, she sensed somethin'. She mentioned he wasn't sleepin'. She kept pushin' on me—so I gave her a hint. Not serious.

                     BOTTS
What "a hint"?

                    MEROLA
"Teeth." That's all I said. Teeth. Like that.

                     BOTTS
Teeth?

                    MEROLA
She took it as a joke. She laughed. It was not pursued. End of discussion. The subject changed. *Never mentioned again.*

    A pause

BOTTS
Then she's still in the dark.

MEROLA
Exactly where she is.

A pause

BOMPKEE
(low)
When was this?

MEROLA
When? The other day.

BOMPKEE
The other day?

MEROLA
You went down for doughnuts. He was out buyin' raincoats.

BOMPKEE
(low)
You sonofabitch.

MEROLA
What?

BOMPKEE
It stops.

MEROLA
Hey, listen I'm bein' up front here, okay? All right?

BOMPKEE
It *stops*.

MEROLA
I'm *reporting* this.

BOMPKEE
Say it. "It stops."

MEROLA
It was a casual remark.
(to Botts)
What?

BOMPKEE
Say it.

MEROLA
You're not hearin' me. Nothin' happened.

BOMPKEE
"Whatever it is, it stops." Say it!

MEROLA
Nothin' happened!

BOMPKEE
Say it! "Whatever it is, it stops!"

MEROLA

Nothin' happened!

BOMPKEE

Say it, whatever it is!

MEROLA

Okay! Whatever it is. It stops.

BOMPKEE

What stops!

MEROLA

Whatever it is.
    (to Botts)
Nothin' happened, for chrissake—

BOMPKEE
(to Botts)

And you stay the hell outta my place when I'm not home!

BOTTS

Are you nuts? Who got you back inside?
    (pause)
And how about you keep the fuck away from my sister!

BOMPKEE

Nothin' happened.
    (pause)
I'm a married man!

(a silence)
Nushkin's probably home takin' a hot bath.

          MEROLA

Fuck fuckin' Nushkin.

          BOTTS

Tomorrow we blow up his car.

          BOMPKEE

Right.

          MEROLA

We *demolish* it.

          BOTTS

We'll get some satisfaction.

    A pause.

          BOMPKEE

What about the heater?

          BOTTS

We hook up the heater, we lose the light.

          BOMPKEE

I've seen enough.

          BOTTS

Let's do it.

He hooks up the space heater, the light dies. The heater throws out a reddish glow.

Who remembers the drill?

MEROLA
One man covers. The rest face the source till your backs get cold, then reverse position.

BOTTS
Like grilled cheese.

They sit beside one another, Bompkee and Botts face the heater. Merola, between them, covers, facing away, as if reliving the feeling. After a moment he turns, joins them facing out.

MEROLA
You know what I thought about every night? My ideal? One hour, alone, gimme one single hour alone with any slim, blond, eighteen-year-old virgin—nymphomaniac.
(thinks)
I built the whole body. Inch by inch. Five-seven. Real green eyes. Hair not absolutely blond, more off-blond. Long. And regular fingernails, with no polish. Always clean—steppin' out from a shower, with a tub, not a stall shower. Steppin' over—
(pause)
I could imagine everything but the face.

(pause)
I came home, I figured if anybody in Jersey could find one, just one, it'd be me. It's never happened. I've arrived at the conclusion that virgins don't exist in New Jersey. *They drive through.*

BOTTS
Where's the refreshments?
(to Merola)
You bought fifteen bucks' worth of food.

MEROLA
It's in the trunk.

BOTTS
What about the pint?

MEROLA
(pulls a pint from his raincoat)
We can't get ten miles from home anymore, why is that?

Botts takes the pint from him opens it, swigs.

BOMPKEE
The last place we travelled was what, D.C. For two days.

BOTTS
That afternoon in D.C. The card game. A very quiet guy. Do you remember him? Red bandanna?

BOMPKEE
The beard?

BOTTS
We took a walk together, Pennsylvania Avenue. This was a good guy. Perez. Harry Perez. He said he'd been through some shit over there.

BOMPKEE
They said he got busted out.

BOTTS
The army had tried to court-martial him. They said he blew away a couple of little slope kids. He told me he saw two kids on a road leading outta some wiped-out duc they'd just swept. Both kids with their intestines hangin' out, moanin' and whimperin'. He got so upset he bent down and took 'em outta their misery. So he gets court-martialed. But, he beats it. He gets an honorable discharge. He's out.
(pause)
Now, a couple days ago I open the paper. I see his picture. Harry Perez! A whole article. The full story.
(pause)
He had come home and? Zero. Nothin'. Nothin' happens for him. He becomes a drifter. Some odd jobs. Nothin' steady. Nothin' works out.
(pause)
So he builds a little shelter near some river. This is a shack. Now he's a bum, right?
(pause)
Three days ago he's sittin' under a bridge with some homeless guy he met, fishin', shootin' rats, drinkin'. They get into a battle. Big fight. Over what? The bottle. The guy reaches, grabs for his twenty-two, blasts a hole through Harry's forehead.

(pause)

Boom. Cleaned. He's gone.

(pause)

We played hearts with this guy. A good guy!

(pause)

No luck.

(pause)

Over and out. He's done. That's his life.

(a beat)

Under some bridge!

(pause)

How the fuck did we get into this, *us*?

MEROLA

Bad luck, poor planning, faulty execution—like that.

BOMPKEE

And shitty ideas.

BOTTS AND MEROLA

Right.

A pause.

MEROLA

You know there is a way—

They look at him.

We sell the ovens; they're almost new. We sell the refrigerators, the freezers, the microwave, the air conditioners—

BOMPKEE

Whatta you talkin' about?

MEROLA

Stools, tables, chairs, glasses, mirrors, light fixtures, sinks, the stock, the shelves, the bar! All of it, we sell everything! Give the cash to Caravelli. It'll be close enough; he'll take it. And we walk away individually. Dissolve the partnership.

BOMPKEE

You wanna dissolve us?

MEROLA

We've been doin' things together how long? Has anything actually worked out?

BOTTS

That leaves us where?

MEROLA

We keep doin' shit like this. It's unhealthy!

BOTTS

No! We've got through a lotta tough situations together. Let's face it, were good at that. But somethin' looks easy, we tend to fuck it up. All I can tell you is, we're due.

MEROLA

Ritchie, please—

BOTTS

Everybody at some point, I don't care if it's a fuckin' cripple, women, Indians, the aged, *everybody* sooner or later catches a goddam break. Believe me, we are due.

MEROLA

I'm sorry, I don't know who's due what anymore.

BOMPKEE

Yeah—
(pause)
I got this weird urge the other day when I was out buyin' us the gloves. All of a sudden I wanted to carry an M-16 into the goddam mall, climb onto a balcony and look over the whole fuckin' enterprise, all the holiday shoppers with their bags fulla shit, everybody "in the spirit."
(pause)
I stand there, I take it in. Then I rip off a clip into the skylight, glass crashin' down, everybody scatters like rats.
(pause)
And then I begin to play a serious game. I start pickin' each one of 'em off in their fuckin' prime! First I take out the men. The assholes carryin' the bags, in their sweat suits, the leather runnin' shoes, divin' for cover. Then I pump their fat-assed wives in jeans, screamin' like rabbits, slidin' across the glass.
(pause)
And that's where I stop.
(emotional)
I leave the kids be!
(overcome)
You should never fuck with the youth of America—

BOTTS
(gently, comforting him)
Hey. The past—is history. That's all behind us. We leave here in the morning, the sun'll be up. We'll get a fresh start. The great thing about this country, you can always get a fresh start—it's what you do with it that counts. Let's remember that.
(optimistic)
Fuck the past.

MEROLA
(bitter)
Fuck the past.

BOMPKEE
(dazed)
Fuck the past.

After a moment, Merola turns, and Botts and Bompkee turn around with him, their backs to the heat. The LIGHTS fade slowly and we are carried into the darkness.

THE END

HAIR OF THE DOG

SCENE ONE

As the house lights fade down, we hear wind and heavy rain. In the dark, Hurricane Sandy roars through the big city—floodwaters surge, high winds scream. It's October, 2012.

After a few beats we shift from the sound of chaos outside to early morning inside a comfortable, stylishly decorated living area of an enormous East Side Manhattan apartment. Suggestions of wealth define the room: sleek furniture, white walls with hanging art and oversize photos of landscapes, high-tech lighting that beams onto pieces of contemporary sculpture in steel and bronze, on pedestals. There's one delicate piece encased in translucent plastic.

Upstage left is the entryway to the family quarters and library. Up right leads to the guest rooms, gym, laundry, sauna. There's a bar with stools down right, and a breakfast nook down left that leads to the offstage kitchen and dining room. There's a hallway to the unseen front door down right of the bar.

It's a shiny safe haven perched above an ongoing calamity.

RICHARD, A trim, fifty-year-old man, stands facing upstage on a cellphone, his back to us. He's got a towel around his neck wearing sweats. He's not getting good news.

RICHARD
(on phone)
Right. Okay.
(deep breath)
Yeah, no I'll be fine, Morty, after I hang myself.
(a beat)
Thanks, Morty.

He ends the call. His body slumps a moment until he hears his wife approaching. Richard straightens up, turns as PHYLLIS enters the room on her cellphone, shaking her head in dismay. Phyllis is dressed in sheik boots, black jeans, black cashmere turtleneck. She's a few years younger than Richard and takes very good care of herself—at any moment, mid-conversation, she might execute a yoga stretch. There's an irrepressible energy and good nature about her that, despite her narrow world view, is hard to resist.

PHYLLIS
(on phone)
No, it's all right, Rosa, I understand, I totally understand. It's very scary out there—but if you change your mind I'll send a car. It's okay—we'll make do. Where do we keep the guest room linens? For all the bathrooms? Okay, all right. I might have to call you if I can't find things. Say hola to Pablo and Ernesto. Bye bye now.
(ends the call, shakes her head)
She said the mayor told her to stay indoors. Maybe I should call him and ask if his help showed up today.

RICHARD
(distracted)
What's this about the guest rooms?

PHYLLIS
I told you I asked my brother and his family. They're on the way, I sent a car.

RICHARD
You said you were thinking of asking them.
(sniffs)
Why do I smell bad fruit?

PHYLLIS
They've lost power, Richard. Everybody south of thirty-fourth street.

RICHARD
The worst storm in a hundred years and we're entertaining.

PHYLLIS
The city's half under water. Family's where you go in a crisis.

RICHARD
An unexamined truism.

PHYLLIS
Oh?

RICHARD

If you want to stay calm in a crisis, maybe family's what you avoid. Okay, don't worry, I'll be gracious. As long as your brother doesn't hound me for another contribution to his "golden circle." He's relentless.

PHYLLIS

Because he's passionate about his work. It's not a fault.

RICHARD

And maybe he'll tell us why your mother's condo hasn't sold.

PHYLLIS
(evasive)

I've got a million things to do.

RICHARD

It's been on the market for ages, hasn't it?

PHYLLIS
(turns to go)

They'll be here—I sent a car.

RICHARD

Phyl—

PHYLLIS
(starts off)

What are the chances I can get Amber to help me make beds?

RICHARD
Phyl?

PHYLLIS
Maybe I shouldn't even bother.

Hearing something in his voice, she turns back.

RICHARD
Morty called.
(*a beat*)
Tomorrow morning. Tomorrow's paper.

PHYLLIS
Tomorrow's paper?
(*she sits*)
Saying what, exactly?

RICHARD
"Subject of an inquiry."

PHYLLIS
That's it, "subject of an inquiry?"

RICHARD
"On possible manipulation of treasury futures."

PHYLLIS
(*up on her feet*)
So, maybe the storm's a good distraction. Nobody'll read about it, it'll be buried.

(goes to him for an extended hug)
And you can exhaust yourself running the marathon tomorrow. Then you'll get involved with your photography—you've got so much talent!

RICHARD
I'll have to tell your brother when they get here.

PHYLLIS
My brother? Why?

RICHARD
They can't read about it at our breakfast table, Phyl.

PHYLLIS
The paper might not even be delivered tomorrow!
(sees him looking at her)
I'm sorry, I just—the thought of people enjoying this boils my blood.

RICHARD
Your brother's not one of them.

PHYLLIS
He's not, right.

RICHARD
We can't do anything about what people think. We'll manage. We know the truth.

PHYLLIS
We'll manage better with the truth and a really good PR person. Please reconsider it. Please?

RICHARD
(nods)
My parents would be mortified.

PHYLLIS
Your parents would be proud of you if you were a serial killer. "He outsmarted the FBI for years!"

RICHARD
My father would be embarrassed.

PHYLLIS
No. He'd be angry at them for embarrassing you. Please just concentrate on your immediate goal—tomorrow's marathon.

RICHARD
They're starting to question it.

PHYLLIS
The mayor is totally supportive. He wants to run it. I just heard him.

RICHARD
My whole system's on go. I'm fine-tuned! I can't just shut myself down—five months of training, all those miles, all that pasta?

                        PHYLLIS
Sweetheart—

                        RICHARD
I'll implode.

                        PHYLLIS
It's just the outer boroughs complaining—and they have no power. Retain focus, stay on message. The immediate goal: eight and a half minute miles.

                        RICHARD
Right. Okay. Thanks, coach.

She gives him a thumbs up, smacks his butt and starts off.

                        PHYLLIS
Sheets and towels, I can do this.
                        (remembers)
Oh! I've got a fabulous idea for my next quilt. As soon as I can finish the one I'm conceptualizing. It's fabulous, like—almost like a tapestry—but I can't talk about it yet.

As she turns to go their daughter, AMBER, twenty, enters left wearing a white surgical mask and blue flannel pajamas. She's looking down at her cellphone as she does a complete 360° turn-around before entering.

Her parents watch. Richard looks at Phyllis, who shrugs.

AMBER
(not looking up from cell)
Where's Rosa?

PHYLLIS
Rosa's staying home because of the storm.

AMBER
But she's all right? I can't deal with more loss.

PHYLLIS
She's fine. But no pancakes. I'm sorry.

Amber, still focused on the cell, turns to go back to her room.

RICHARD
Amber, what's with the surgical mask?

Phyllis wishes he hadn't asked.

AMBER
Two reasons. One, there's an intensely unpleasant fruit smell in here. Ask Mom about that. And two, hantavirus protection.

RICHARD
Hantavirus. Isn't that about mice?

PHYLLIS
With the death of Creamy, Amber feels at risk visiting us without her cat.

RICHARD
But we don't have mice.
(looks at Phyllis, who shrugs)
So get yourself another cat.

PHYLLIS
Way too soon!
(uh-oh)

AMBER
How insensitive can you be, Dad?

RICHARD
(raises his hands)
Sorry! I'm really—

AMBER
Animals have large souls.

RICHARD
I forgot the time frame. You know I was fond of Creamy.

Amber shakes her head in pity.

PHYLLIS
(to Amber)
Will you help me make up the guest rooms?

AMBER
Their lives have meaning.

Richard nods, chastened

Is this like a mother-daughter thing, or an actual necessity?

PHYLLIS
A necessity. Uncle Wolf and the family. They've lost power.

AMBER
Okay. Wow, they've got a great Siamese.
(realizes)
Aunt Rhoda as your house-guest? This must be a real emergency.

Phyllis nods.

Hey, courageous, Mom. I'm impressed.

PHYLLIS
Thank you.
(points her upstage right)
I'll be right there. Towels and washcloths on the beds, please.

Amber, head down on the cell, exits up right.

RICHARD
I thought we were done with the—spinning.

PHYLLIS
The loss of Creamy was a setback.

RICHARD
Apparently so.

PHYLLIS
She's almost ready to start the search process, but it won't be easy. She wants a kitten related to Creamy, even distantly.

RICHARD
She'll need a cat genealogist.

PHYLLIS
I told her she should stay here until she feels comfortable going back to her place.

RICHARD
Absolutely.

PHYLLIS
She says she's not ready yet. She can't face an empty apartment and the clean litter box.

He nods. She exits to the guest rooms upstage right. Richard stands still a moment evaluating his morning so far. He suddenly begins running vigorously in place, legs pumping for five seconds and then stops. Just as he starts again, an intercom sounds. He stops, goes towards the front hallway off right and presses a button.

RICHARD
(on intercom)
Yes, what is it? Send them up, Tony. Tell them the door's open. Thank you.

He turns back into the room and immediately sprints in place again. His cell phone rings; he stops running, answers it.

Hello. Who is this? How did you get this number? No comment. No comment!

Agitated, he ends the call and does an even more energetic sprint in place. When he stops, he exits left, slowly, resigned, towards the bedrooms.

After a couple beats a WOMAN'S HEAD, covered in a black hijab, only eyes visible, peers into the room from the unseen hallway, right. Then she disappears.

MAN'S VOICE
Hello, everybody! We're here. The refugees have arrived!

A tubby man, WOLF, around fifty, is followed inside by his sturdy wife, RHODA, both overwhelmed by large, yellow rain slickers, rain hats, and big black rubber boots. Behind them is their daughter, BECCA, twenty, totally covered up in the hijab and a long, black burka. She's followed by her twenty-something boyfriend FRANCISCO, underdressed in tight black jeans, sneakers, a short leather jacket, and a white T-shirt.

Wolf and Rhoda lug suitcases, Becca has a large shoulder bag. Francisco's got his laptop. They stand silently a moment, taking in the glittery living room.

FRANCISCO
Something smells.

BECCA
God, what am I doing here?

FRANCISCO
Like bad fucking fruit.

WOLF
Francisco, please.

FRANCISCO
Sorry Wolf, but the place stinks.

WOLF
Not here, all right?

BECCA
Dad, don't squelch him. He's allowed to express himself.

WOLF
We're guests, Becca. And he's our guest.

BECCA
Truth can't be the prisoner of circumstance.

Wolf and Rhoda exchange a look of parental pride.

FRANCISCO
I like that! Thanks.

Becca raises the hijab and kisses him enthusiastically.

                              WOLF

We were here just a few months ago—it's all new stuff, new objects d'art.

                              RHODA
                           (to Francisco)

Wolf's sister "collects."

                              WOLF

And she quilts. She's on the museum board.

                           FRANCISCO

So is this a showroom or a living room? Or a bank?

                              BECCA

The city's on its knees and we visit Park Avenue.

                              RHODA

Becca, please.

                              BECCA

I don't want to be here, Mom.

                              RHODA

We are staying put.

                              BECCA

This visit is perverse! We're supposed to sit on our butts and drink lattes? People need help.

FRANCISCO
(interested)
They make lattes here?

BECCA
(to her parents)
I don't get it, you used to be involved. You were activists.

Phyllis, as she enters up right, speaks loudly behind her, offstage.

PHYLLIS
(to Amber, unseen)
Please fold the towels on each bed, at the foot of the beds.

She stops, seeing them; does a double take at Francisco and the covered-up woman

Oh! Look who's here—hello!

WOLF
(embraces his sister)
The doorman sent us up.

PHYLLIS
Hello! Of course. Take off your rain gear, leave it in the hall closet. What a disaster out there!

RHODA
(kisses her)
Thanks so much for having us, Phyllis.

PHYLLIS
Isn't it awful?

WOLF
The place looks great, Phyl.

He and Rhoda remove their slickers.

PHYLLIS
Thank you!

FRANCISCO
(to Becca)
Total bullshit.

WOLF
Phyl, this is Becca's friend Francisco. I hope it's okay, he had nowhere to go.

FRANCISCO
I'm a loser.

PHYLLIS
Of course, of course. How do you do, Francisco?

FRANCISCO
How do I do? How do you do? Should we shake hands?

PHYLLIS
(confused)
Okay, sure. And this is?

(shakes)

FRANCISCO
(to himself)
"Shaking hands."

BECCA
It's me, Aunt Phyl.

PHYLLIS
Becca? Oh, I'm so relieved.

BECCA
Who did you think it was?

PHYLLIS
Well, I had no idea! A new housekeeper?

RHODA
Becca's been researching oppressed women.

WOLF
Boots on the ground.

PHYLLIS
Is this for a course?

FRANCISCO
The burka brigade.

               BECCA
          (nods to Phyllis)
I'm trying to understand how it feels to be universally ignored or condescended to.

               PHYLLIS
Oh. And how does it feel?

               BECCA
It's infuriating. And seriously uncomfortable.

> *She lets the burka drop to the floor. She's wearing black leggings, black shorts, and a pink T-shirt.*

I can't believe these poor women. Every time they step outdoors—extreme heat, extreme cold, wet, stifling—all because of crazy men.
          (remembers)
Oh.

> *She pulls off the hijab, flashing a big, warm grin.*

It's really me!

> *She hugs her aunt.*

               AMBER'S VOICE
Mom, the blue towels go better on the paisley bed spreads.

> *In her mask, she enters right and does a 360°. They watch her, she looks up.*

Hi.

     WOLF & RHODA
     (go to her)

Amber! Hi sweetheart!

     BECCA

Hey, Amber. This is Francisco.

 Amber waves to him.

     FRANCISCO

Hey. What's up with the mask?

     BECCA

You sick?

     AMBER

I'm sick of the smell.

     FRANCISCO

Really.

     BECCA

Yeah, we noticed.

     WOLF

What smell?

     RHODA

Is there a smell?

PHYLLIS
(bothered, points to a sculpture)
This piece is by Hogens Watt, one of the country's foremost unrecognized sculptors.

WOLF
Is that what smells, Phyl?

PHYLLIS
It's extremely valuable and we have it on consideration for two weeks.

AMBER
A plastic, porthole casing embedded with slowly rotting fruit.

PHYLLIS
It's a statement.

FRANCISCO
What's the statement?

AMBER
The soul of America is like slowly rotting fruit.

RHODA
(ironic)
I'm surprised he isn't better known.

PHYLLIS
He will be.

BECCA
And if not, he can always get a job at Whole Foods.

FRANCISCO
You're going to buy that?

PHYLLIS
We haven't decided.

AMBER
Dad just started smelling it this morning.

PHYLLIS
(lifting it)
You know, I think I'll just take this inside for now.
   (to Wolf and Rhoda)
Come with me and get settled. Richard's showering.

They pick up their bags.

AMBER
Where's your cat?

Becca slaps her forehead.

Oh no! You forgot her?

BECCA
Kidding! She's by the front door. Should I get her?

Amber nods, Becca exits to the hallway.

PHYLLIS
(low)
What are the—arrangements?

RHODA
They sleep together, why pretend?

As they exit right.

PHYLLIS
Amber, when they're ready bring them inside.

AMBER
(to Francisco)
You're Candy Rocks. I recognize you from The Cave.

FRANCISCO
No kidding?

BECCA
(Enters with cat in carrier)
Here's Ziggy!

FRANCISCO
She knows Candy Rocks.

BECCA
(points to him)
The best DJ in America. Numero Uno.

                    FRANCISCO
She got that right.

                    AMBER
Ziggy looks miserable.

                    BECCA
She's in a cage.

                    FRANCISCO
I used to do three-sixties.

                    BECCA
Dude, you never told me that.

                    FRANCISCO
For almost a year.

                    AMBER
What made you stop?

                    FRANCISCO
I got a dog. That was it. I never felt the need again. Weird, right?

                    AMBER
My cat died two weeks ago.

                    BECCA
Creamy died?

FRANCISCO
That hurts.

BECCA
You want Ziggy in your room?

AMBER
Can I?

BECCA
Sure. I gotta go pee. Your bathroom okay?

Amber nods, picks up the carrier and looks at Ziggy as Becca exits left.

FRANCISCO
So you go to The Cave a lot?

AMBER
(staring at the cat)
Just twice. I loved the music but I couldn't stand the body odor. I thought your mixes were amazing. There was a real creative mind behind that program. At first your choices seemed arbitrary, even contradictory, but by the end it was very satisfying, musically.

FRANCISCO
Oh. Thanks. You blog about music?
(She shakes her head, No.)

You should. You've got insights.

AMBER

I'm more into felines.

FRANCISCO

How do you live here?

AMBER

What do you mean?

FRANCISCO

This place is ridiculous. You can't get any perspective—it's like living inside a wallet.

AMBER

I have my own apartment.
(points at laptop)
Is that how you do your mixes, on the laptop? All the music's in there?

FRANCISCO
(nods, points to his head)
And here. So did you lose power, too?

AMBER

No. I lost my cat.
(turns for her bedroom with the cat carrier)
Hey, Ziggy, everything's okay. You can stay with me.

She exits left. Francisco looks around, alone in the big space. He moves in for a closer take on the sculptures, picks up a long, bronze object, hefts it, puts it down as Richard enters left, in slacks and button-down.

                        RICHARD
                    (with bonhomie)
Hello there! Welcome.

                       FRANCISCO
Hey.

                        RICHARD
                   (extends a hand)
I'm Uncle Richard.

      Amused, Francisco shakes his hand.

Amber said I should say hello to "Candy Rocks." What's that mean?

                       FRANCISCO
What's it mean?
                        (shrugs)
I'm Francisco.

                        RICHARD
So it's some sort of stage name?

                       FRANCISCO
DJ.

RICHARD
Oh, on the radio. You play songs.

FRANCISCO
Mixes. I work clubs.

RICHARD
Mixes. Educate me, Francisco.

FRANCISCO
Sounds—chunks from existing sources, pulled together, cuts reprogrammed into new, the new.

RICHARD
(a beat)
There must be legal issues involved with all that.

FRANCISCO
(grins)
As if you knew what the fuck you were talking about.

RICHARD
(stunned)
What?

FRANCISCO
Why do "adults" assume they know shit? Just because they have stuff? My parents are like that, too.

Wolf enters, right.

WOLF

Richard!

RICHARD

Good to see you, Wolf.

Richard moves to greet him with a quick look back at Francisco, who drops into a chair, opens his laptop and disappears into it.

WOLF

Good to be here, believe me. There are some things it's no fun to do with a flashlight.

RICHARD
(low, indicating Francisco)

What's with—

WOLF
(nods)

We'll talk. Listen, I'm sorry about this inquiry. You'll get past it and move on.

RICHARD
(surprised)

Phyllis told you.

WOLF

I think she was anxious it shouldn't fester, you know? It's terrible what they're doing, going after good people. There isn't enough real crime? I hear it all the time now—well, not all the time, but some of our most generous contributors, believe me.

RICHARD
How about a coffee, some juice?

WOLF
Sure, soon. Amber looks well, what I could see of her.

RICHARD
She's doing okay. Her cat died.

WOLF
So she wears a mask?

RICHARD
A long story. I just got a big greeting from Becca—she looks great.

WOLF
Believe me—Becca has her own disguises.

RICHARD
And how's the hate business?

Becca enters left, moves to Francisco.

WOLF
(with a grin)
Unfortunately, we're busy. Incidents in the U.S. are up. Even though in most places it's no longer acceptable to spout bigotry.

But nobody's fooled. I tell young people anti-Semitism is the Dracula of bigotry. It won't die, you can't kill it.

BECCA
(looks up)
His organization started out protecting American Jews, now it's a shill for a foreign country.

WOLF
(to Richard, re Becca)
The perils of a free-speech home environment.

BECCA
It's an Israel lobby. That's how it gets all its "support."

WOLF
(re Becca)
We have a difference of opinion but somehow manage to coexist.

BECCA
One's an opinion, one's the truth.

WOLF
Juvenile demagoguery.

FRANCISCO
(low to Becca)
Versus old farts.

Becca laughs, the two men glance over, sensing it. Francisco gives them a thumbs up. Richard looks at Wolf, perplexed by Francisco.

WOLF
Francisco's an original. My apartment is crawling with them.

Phyllis and Rhoda enter right, talking.

PHYLLIS
Richard's been training every morning for months—Central Park, six a.m..

RHODA
Obsessive behavior can be very impressive.

RICHARD
Wolf, how do you stay so calm? I can't imagine.

WOLF
(smiles)
That's my job—moderation at home and abroad.

PHYLLIS
Richard, I'm afraid the mayor is starting to waver.

RICHARD
He won't buckle.

RHODA
Staten Island is flooded. It's a superstorm. Queens is devastated.

RICHARD
There's too much at stake.

RHODA
He's got to listen to his constituents, Richard. They're angry.

RICHARD
The marathon's uplifting, a spiritual boost, an escape. Turn your back for a couple hours, cheer on your friends, hand water bottles to strangers—with all the anguish going on it's a positive, unifying event.

BECCA
(ironic)
And really good for business.

RICHARD
It brings the city millions, yes.

FRANCISCO
A commercial bonanza.

RICHARD
That's not to be sneezed at.

BECCA
Just barfed at.

RHODA
Becca.

BECCA
No. Haven't you been watching, Uncle Richard? People need help, not handing out water bottles.

RICHARD
Becca, the marathon has become a great New York tradition.

BECCA
Well, I think all traditions are suspect.

RICHARD
In times of trouble, traditions are a foundation.

BECCA
Then they should pass a relevance test. We don't go to hangings anymore, that was a tradition.

FRANCISCO
Bear baiting was a good one.

BECCA
Everything that's blindly accepted should questioned.

RICHARD
(enjoying her)
For instance?

BECCA
For instance people still worship the military.

FRANCISCO

"The military."

RICHARD

Because it's protected us for two hundred and fifty years.

BECCA

It can't protect its own women!

RICHARD

True. Apparently not yet. But it still stands between us and chaos.

BECCA

I'm not talking about its utility, Uncle Richard, I'm talking about its being worshipped.

PHYLLIS

How about some coffee! Who's ready?

BECCA

So much money spent on weapon systems while people are hungry? Homeless? It's just another dumb tradition—blind flag worship. You'd think everyone in uniform was an angel.

FRANCISCO

Just another job with benefits.

WOLF

No. It's a lot more than just a job, Francisco.

RICHARD

It's service. Honorable service.

FRANCISCO

Okay, woman-abusing honorable service.

RICHARD

Oh, for god's sake!

PHYLLIS

What about food? You guys were up so early.

WOLF

Coffee sounds good to me.

RHODA

I'd love some.

PHYLLIS

Kids? We've got eggs, toast, cereal.

FRANCISCO

Anything—non-traditional?

He's broken the tension as Amber steps into the room doing her three-sixty spin. They all watch her.

AMBER
(cautiously)

Dad?

RICHARD

Yes, sweetheart?

AMBER
(concerned for him)

They just cancelled the marathon.

RICHARD
(with a look at Phyllis)

Excuse me.

He exits left. An uncomfortable silence.

AMBER
(lifts up surgical mask)

You know...
(inhales)

It's starting to smell okay in here.

She removes the mask: a big, winning grin.

LIGHTS DROP

SCENE TWO

About an hour later. Phyllis and Wolf sit down left, having coffee. Francisco, still on his laptop, has sunk deeper into the chair.

PHYLLIS

He's been very stoic. I know the injustice of it eats at him, but somehow he's able to compartmentalize. That's a rare skill, believe me. Bill Clinton—I don't know how he did it. The whole country, the whole world knew he'd been getting those blow jobs in the Oval Office, but he managed to stand there with a straight face and talk about the economy—as if nobody was snickering! Well, Richard can do that, too. He'll push it aside, make money, and let the lawyers handle it. But now there's no marathon to distract him, and tomorrow he's going to be fingered in the business section. I mean featured. It's so unfair. He creatively discovered a new business approach, a very useful tool, but because it hadn't been seen on the street before they go after him. He's just smarter and they resent that.

WOLF

It must be tough on you, too.

PHYLLIS

Well, he's got his photography. Oh, I'll be abandoned. I know it. My so-called friends. One whiff of embarrassment. It's like—like a wine stain on a wedding dress. Even if somebody spilled on you and it's not your fault, you'll still have to throw it out, the entire dress! Not that you'd ever wear it again.

WOLF

This is excellent coffee.

PHYLLIS

Thank you. It's one of the few things I can still manage in the kitchen. Rosa's so good all my culinary skills have atrophied. It's a real loss.

WOLF

You know, Phyl, we really should talk about Mom's condo while we're together.

PHYLLIS

Please, Wolf. With all that's going on?

WOLF

I know, I know—

PHYLLIS
(realizes)

They could force me off the board! Museums hate controversy. And we've done nothing wrong!
(shakes her head)
They never investigate plain vanilla people, and I'm not pointing fingers but people cheat on their taxes, they all do it. Rosa does it! We have never cheated, not once. We just pay less—which is perfectly legal.

WOLF

There's no point jumping to conclusions about the museum, Phyl.

PHYLLIS
And suppose, god forbid, he's indicted, or convicted! Then what happens? Even house arrest—Martha Stewart got that. He'd be here twenty-four seven wearing one of those hideous ankle bracelets.

Rhoda enters from the kitchen with coffee.

RHODA
(sits)
Should we check on Richard, is he all right?

WOLF
He'll be fine. Phyl says he'll focus on his cameras.

RHODA
What about a therapist—to get him through this?

PHYLLIS
I wonder if house arrest allows you to visit your vacation home? I mean is there a second-home provision?
(a beat)
A therapist? You could suggest it, but stand back.

RHODA
Or a minister? That church you go to—do you still go?

PHYLLIS
He's not a religious person, you know that.

RHODA
(shrugs)
Well, times of stress. I could recommend a colleague.

WOLF
He's got a mind like a steel trap, he'll be okay.

RHODA
Pushing things down is not a solution, Wolf, you know that. I hope you know that by now.

WOLF
People handle stress differently.

RHODA
I was simply making a suggestion.

Becca enters with toast.

BECCA
Staten Island is so clobbered. Those poor people.
(calls over to him)
Francisco? Let's do breakfast.
(to others)
The mayor's talking again. I can't stand him. Such a know-it-all, with that little cashmere swagger.
(to Phyllis)
Amber said you're doing this massive quilt about grandma—that sounds amazing.

Francisco comes over, she puts her arms around him and they start to exit left to the kitchen.

PHYLLIS
Thank you Becca, I hope so!

WOLF
A quilt about Mom?

PHYLLIS
It's a concept—her illness.

WOLF
Her illness?

PHYLLIS
The stages of it.

RHODA
So—it's a—quilt about cancer?

Phyllis nods.

How does that work?

PHYLLIS
It's—there are connected sections, of her journey: Discomfort, Discovery, X-Rays, Surgery, Pain, Radiation, Hair loss, Nausea, Courage, Perseverance, Morphine, Hallucination—Love.

A beat.

WOLF
Wow. And you're sewing all this?

PHYLLIS
I'm describing it. It's still a concept at the moment.

WOLF
And then you—

RHODA
Are there drawings, sketches?

PHYLLIS
There will be.

RHODA
So you'll—

WOLF
I didn't know you could draw, Phyl.

PHYLLIS
I'm interviewing.

RHODA
Who are you interviewing?

PHYLLIS
Artisans.

A pause.

RHODA

An artisan will do the drawings?

Phyllis nods.

WOLF

Then you'll do the sewing?

PHYLLIS

I don't sew. I'm a conceptualist. I'll interview.

RHODA

A different—artisan.

PHYLLIS
(nods)

There's a collective.

RHODA

So—you're essentially outsourcing the cancer quilt?

PHYLLIS
(rises with her cup)

No. I don't see it that way.

She exits to the kitchen. Wolf shakes his head.

RHODA

She's a what?

WOLF

Did you really have to say that, "outsourcing"?

RHODA

I was just trying to understand. It's bizarre. A cancer quilt? And she's a "conceptualist"?

WOLF

And why bring up church, the minister? Really, Rhoda.

RHODA

That's where she goes, isn't it?

WOLF

I don't ask where she goes.

RHODA

Should I have suggested a rabbi, would that have been well-received?

WOLF

Therapist was more than enough.

RHODA

She's been going to church for years. Isn't she comfortable with it?

WOLF

It's none of our business.

RHODA
Amber doesn't even think she's Jewish.

WOLF
She's not.

RHODA
Well, if her mother was born—

WOLF
Stop. It's America. You can be whatever you want. Could we please stop this now?

Becca enters looking at her cellphone, Francisco behind her looking at his.

BECCA
Aunt Phyl's in there crying at the stove. What did you say to her?

RHODA
Oh, god.

FRANCISCO
She's overcooking my cheese omelette.

RHODA
She's the one who needs therapy.

BECCA
Mom! You said that? About disowning her heritage? You're a psychologist.

RHODA
No, of course I didn't say it.

WOLF
(rises)
I better talk to her.

RHODA
No. I'll—I'll speak with her.

WOLF
Not yet. I need to prep her first.

He exits into the kitchen.

BECCA
Daddy the fixer.

FRANCISCO
But can he fix my omelette?

RHODA
We should've stayed home in the dark.

FRANCISCO
An innocent omelette victimized by family bullshit.

BECCA
It's really upsetting to see your aunt cry.

FRANCISCO
(looks up at entertainment unit)
Is there any room in this place without a TV?

RHODA
She cries easily. So did their mother—she cried when they were out of toilet paper.

BECCA
You know—I've been trying to understand—what's the relative value of tears?
(points up at TV)
Those people on the news, they've lost everything—their houses, clothes, family photos, possessions—and Aunt Phyl, who has everything, crying about an insult.

RHODA
A perceived insult.

BECCA
There's all sorts of tears, you know, from different emotions. I wonder if the tear chemistry changes—I mean if it's from a deeper pain.

FRANCISCO
Dude, maybe you should switch majors—get into science and shit.

RHODA
She has a highly inquisitive mind, but it's not a scientific mind.

>   *(rises)*
I better go make nice.

>   *She exits to the kitchen.*

>   BECCA
>   *(amazed)*
She thinks she knows what kind of mind I have!

>   FRANCISCO
She's so full of it. Too many advanced degrees.
>   *(points to TV)*
Those are some real tears, right there.

>   BECCA
Dude, they're all real.

>   *A silence, both looking up at the TV. Becca glances towards the kitchen.*

She's jealous of all this, but she'll never admit it. God. I see it with Aunt Phyl, too—they have these—animosities. From years of being bothered by stupid, petty stuff. Years and years of it.
>   *(shakes her head)*
And they can't shake it. Maybe it's like—it gets so familiar it's like comforting, you know? Jealousy, distrust, dislike—even if it started about squat, they won't let it go. It's like a mantra, "I can't stand her, I can't stand him." Everybody's pathetic "family history."
>   *(a beat)*
You've got to be on guard all the time—against habit.

A silence as they look up at the TV.

FRANCISCO
You think we'll know each other in five years?

BECCA
(a beat)
There isn't much of a shelf-life for twenty-something relationships. So—probably not.
He nods. They keep looking up.

LIGHTS DROP

SCENE THREE

Just before noon. Down right at the bar, Richard pours Wolf a drink, and one for himself. Rhoda, in a chair nearby, reads. Francisco and his lap top are at the breakfast nook, down left.

RICHARD
(despairing)
The next six to eight months?

WOLF
Richard, you've got the best—the most powerful attorneys in New York.

RICHARD
Maybe I'll rent a little studio. I've fantasized about that. Just take pictures, practice my art.

Francisco glances up, hearing the phrase.

RHODA
Are you drinking, Wolfie?

WOLF
Rhoda, this bourbon is best appreciated round the clock. Am I right, Richard?

RICHARD
I find if you start early enough it operates like a slow gathering tsunami—by evening the entire landscape has been obliterated. Care to join us?

RHODA
You make it sound irresistible.

RICHARD
(pours a drink, brings it to Rhoda)
There's no going back, Rhoda.

Becca enters right with an IPad.

BECCA
Wow, early boozing. Totally out of character, Mom.

RHODA
(raises her glass)
Desperate times demand desperate measures.

BECCA
Doesn't seem all that desperate around here to me.
(drops into a couch, opens IPad)
What do decadent times demand?

WOLF
(confidentially)
You know, Richard, strategically thinking, this might be a good moment to make another generous contribution to the organization, our Golden Circle.

RICHARD
(ironic)

I was wondering about that.

WOLF
(missing it)

For you and for us. Beneficial all around. I've been speaking to the White House—it's global. Countries in turmoil, desperate for a scapegoat—blame their inabilities, misfortunes. And the scapegoat? Israel. Got to be the Jews, always Israel at fault.

BECCA
(stands near Francisco)

They ask for it, Dad.

WOLF
(ignores it)

But an aggressive, assertive scapegoat?

BECCA

The neighborhood bully.

WOLF

No! They make mistakes. Dumb, arrogant mistakes, yes. But the country must exist! So I support them, warts and all. There's no alternative.

BECCA

How about criticizing them once in a while.

WOLF

I don't do things halfway. And neither does my daughter. The old days my predecessor could raise enough money just fighting anti-Semitism, with a little civil rights on the side to please the Black community. Then they got themselves going and turned their backs on us, on the entire Jewish community. I understand that, people don't want to feel indebted. But today if you don't carry on big-time for Israel, in the Jewish community you're finished as a player, as a fundraiser. Dead in the water.

BECCA

So you admit it?

WOLF

I'm a realist! So, Richard—a large gift during these difficult days? It will appear selfless, believe me, truly selfless.

RICHARD

And in whose eyes would I appear most selfless, Wolf, God's or the Jews?

WOLF

I can't speak for Him, but certainly for us.

RICHARD

If they indict me would you have to return the gift?

WOLF

I can't believe it'll come to that.

                    RICHARD
I can smell their breath! They smear me, humiliate me—they want to string me up by the testicles. So—would you still want my money, balls flapping in the wind?

                    WOLF
Well—that's a hypothetical. I'd have to ask my board.

                    RICHARD
It's all about how it would "play"?

                    WOLF
No. Not—not entirely, but—maybe you'd be more comfortable holding off. For a while.

                    RICHARD
Maybe I would.

          He pours himself more bourbon. Becca looks up from the couch.

                    BECCA
Why are they so after you, Uncle Richard?

                    RICHARD
Because I offend the limited intelligence of the "regulatory" experts. They resent not having realized it was possible to use the speed in the system to an investor's advantage. And they need to make an example of me to justify their incompetence. Pathetic "watchdog" existence—if they could earn a living they wouldn't need "regulatory" jobs.

> BECCA

But don't we need more regulation? I mean that's what Dad says, curbs and regulations?

> RICHARD

No. Overregulation acts like a chokehold on growth.

> BECCA

That's kind of a Republican mantra, right? "Chokehold on growth."

> RICHARD

Becca, historically the financial markets operate best when left to operate freely. They tend to self-regulate over time.

> BECCA

Like during the meltdown? I mean Bear Whatayacallit and Lehman Dudes self-regulate and kerplop! Down goes the ship.

> RICHARD
> *(patient with her)*

Real-estate stupidity and the housing fiasco ignited the meltdown, Becca, not the stock market.

> BECCA

Okay.
> *(shrugs)*

I thought it had to do with unregulated banks gorging themselves on those terrible mortgage things nobody could understand or pronounce.

                    WOLF
Becca, this is very complex stuff.

                    FRANCISCO
"Bundled instruments!"

                    BECCA
Obviously, Dad.

                    FRANCISCO
Nobody knew jack-shit.

                    BECCA
               (to Wolf and Rhoda)
I don't understand why the two of you—all you talk about reading the *Times* and watching PBS is "regulation, more regulation." Now just because we're up here with Uncle Richard who has a very different take on it, you clam up and let me do the talking. So—am I the ventriloquist or the dummy?

                    FRANCISCO
Dummy!
                    (low voice)
Ventriloquist!
                    (high voice)
Dummy!
                    (low voice)
Ventriloquist!

Becca laughs. Amber appears left, does her three-sixty spin, enters and sits next to Francisco. She looks at his laptop as he works.

RICHARD
(amused)
Becca, would you like some bourbon?

BECCA
I think alcohol's poison, Uncle Richard, but thanks for the offer.

RICHARD
Candy Rocks?

BECCA
He's AA.

FRANCISCO
(not looking up)
I know it's poison.

RICHARD
How long have you been AA, if I may ask?

FRANCISCO
I was sixteen.
(looks up)
Would you like to come to a meeting with me?

Rhoda shakes her head in disbelief.

WOLF
He's incorrigible.

FRANCISCO
Wolf, I might be saving the man's life, you never know.

RICHARD
No, I appreciate the thought, I do.

FRANCISCO
Any time. I mean it. It's hard to go alone.

AMBER
I'll have a shot, Dad.

Richard looks at her, surprised.

Come on, you offered it to Becca.

RICHARD
You really think that's a good idea?

AMBER
Better than drinking alone.

BECCA
(knows what's coming)
Uh-oh—

RHODA
Amber, sweetheart, have you been drinking alone?

WOLF
Rhoda.

BECCA
Don't start analyzing her, Mom.

RHODA
Please—there could be ramifications here.

AMBER
I'm in mourning for my cat, Aunt Rhoda.

Becca stifles a laugh.

RHODA
Oh. I see.

She looks at Richard who shrugs, drinks.

FRANCISCO
Hey, Amber, maybe it's time to move on, you know?

AMBER
Yeah, I guess. I'm about ready. I've been online researching Creamy's relatives.

BECCA
Think bigger. Imagine all the strays out there after this storm.

AMBER
Strays?

BECCA
Wet, cold, hungry?

AMBER
I hadn't thought about strays.

FRANCISCO
Expand your horizons, dude.

BECCA
Really. There's a world beyond Creamy. I mean it's an animal kingdom, right?

AMBER
Right.

BECCA
There's a petition I just signed, to the government of Tanzania. They get kickbacks from poachers. Elephants are being decimated, whole families of them. You can't believe the photos.

AMBER
I saw those photos.

BECCA
I threw up! Killing entire herds for their tusks. What dicks! And rhino, too, because Chinese men want to eat ground-up horns. They think they'll get bigger erections.

RHODA
(nods)
Short men.

BECCA
Mom, it has nothing to do with their height.

RHODA
I think it could.

FRANCISCO
Now she's analyzing Chinese men.

BECCA
We might occupy their UN embassy. I mean once the water recedes. Or we'll go to Washington.

AMBER
I don't have good joining skills. And I might have a travel phobia.

BECCA
And the Japanese—they won't stop killing whales. They're such hypocrites—they say it's for research but they sell whale steaks and whale sushi!

WOLF
Did you know your niece was part of Occupy Wall Street?

BECCA
I was a wuss.

RICHARD
(raises his glass)
Well, their commitment was impressive. I'm not surprised.

BECCA
I came home for showers.

RICHARD
But did you accomplish your goals?

BECCA
Well, if the goal was to change the way the country works—screwing the poor and benefitting the rich, no. But if the goal was to make more people aware of obscene corporate greed—maybe. Maybe it accomplished something. Turns out the FBI had us under surveillance as "anarchist threats."

WOLF
You stood up for what you believed in.

RICHARD
Candy Rocks, you were involved, too?

FRANCISCO
No.

BECCA
He has a hard time believing in anything.

RICHARD
That must make for an interesting relationship.

RHODA
It certainly does.

BECCA
Mom, we connect on many levels.

FRANCISCO
I can only think of two.

RHODA
Please, nothing vivid!

BECCA
Sex and more sex?

They laugh.

RHODA
Oh, god, how much can I take?

Amber rises, exits into kitchen.

BECCA
(concerned)
You think we grossed her out?

FRANCISCO
(not looking up)
We grossed me out.

As Becca exits after Amber, Phyllis enters up right in a large white bathrobe, her head wrapped in a towel.

PHYLLIS
I recommend the sauna, everybody! It's a great mood-changer. You get rid of toxins and your body just—vibrates!

WOLF
Used to be known as a schvitz.

FRANCISCO
(looks up)
How big is it?

PHYLLIS
Big enough for two.

RHODA
(to Francisco)
Oh no!

FRANCISCO
You and me, Rhoda?

Wolf, Richard laugh. Rhoda glares at Wolf.

PHYLLIS
We've got lots of fluffy robes. So we've started drinking, have we?

RICHARD
Did you hit the off-switch, Phyl?

                    PHYLLIS
                    (realizes)
Uh-oh.

    She starts back.

                    RICHARD
                    (Exiting right)
I'll get it. I want to check my cameras. It stopped raining, I might take a walk.

                    PHYLLIS
A walk?
                    (shakes her head)
So—can I get anybody anything? Or, better yet, just go, help yourselves. There's plenty to snack on.

                    WOLF
                    (hesitant)
Phyl, I emailed you that offer on the condo, the latest offer. Did you see it?

                    PHYLLIS
I saw it.

                    RHODA
It looked like a decent offer.

                    PHYLLIS
It was insulting.

A beat.

                    WOLF
You say that about every offer.

                    PHYLLIS
                    (shrugs)
Because it's true.

                    RHODA
Well, they're in the ballpark. Every offer.

                    PHYLLIS
The agent's ballpark. She just wants a sale—so she low-balled the estimate.

                    WOLF
But that's why we got so many estimates up front.

                    PHYLLIS
They all low ball! It's in their interest.

                    WOLF
Phyl, it's been on the market seven months. You've turned down five solid offers.

                    RHODA
Six.

                    WOLF
How long are we—

PHYLLIS

As long as it takes. I will not have my mother's memory insulted. Excuse me, I don't want to catch a chill.

She exits left.

RHODA

She spent her adult life being cruel to her mother—now she equates a sale offer with an insult to her memory.
(shakes her head)
It's interesting. A little scary.

Richard enters carrying a camera and an enormous telephoto lens.

RHODA

Wow, look at that.

WOLF

That is some piece of equipment, Richard.

RHODA

I bet they don't come much bigger than that.

RICHARD

It's all professional grade.

RHODA

Very impressive.

WOLF
Richard, could we speak to you a moment about Mom's condo?

RICHARD
Sure. I've been wondering why you guys just don't sell it.

WOLF
(surprised)
Well, we've been trying. We've had six offers.

RICHARD
Six? Ballpark offers?

They nod.

So what's the problem?

RHODA
Phyllis.

WOLF
She's turned them all down.

RICHARD
Phyl has? Really?

WOLF
I can show you the offers.

RICHARD
Why has she turned them down?

RHODA

She seems to have her own ballpark.

RICHARD

Oh.

(considers)

Okay, I'll speak to her.

(turns to go, stops)

What do you think this is about?

WOLF

It seems complicated.

RHODA

Guilt.

Richard takes that in, heads off left for the bedrooms. Francisco looks up, grins at the size of the lens. Wolf pours himself more bourbon.

WOLF

Maybe he can talk some sense.

RHODA
(extends her glass for more)

I wouldn't bet on it.

Wolf pours her some.

He's become such a Republican. When we first met he was a real human being.

They sip.

                    WOLF
               (looks around)
You know, I feel like I'm having a drink in Bloomingdales.

                   RHODA
Did you see the bath towels? They must be four inches thick.

                    WOLF
I like a thick towel.

    A beat.

                   RHODA
This bourbon is truly superb.

                    WOLF
Very smooth.
               (looks at his glass)
Some of my biggest contributors—
               (shakes his head)
Self-made men, some are serious boozers.
               (a finger over his lips)
Alcoholics! They cycle in and out—hit the red zone, go dry out fancy for a couple weeks, come back make more money. I put up with them, real schmucks—but they're my schmucks. Where would the community be without rich schmucks? You accept the good with the not-so-good—flatter, fund-raise, you navigate, keep moving towards the goal—the yearly goal.

RHODA

Wolfie.

(he looks at her, she grins)

You want to try the sauna?

WOLF

Really? A schvitz?

RHODA
(rising)

When in Rome.

WOLF

The last schvitz I had was with my father.

RHODA

This will be different.

She finishes her drink. They exit right. Francisco, alone in the room, looks up.

LIGHTS DROP

SCENE FOUR

Just after noon. Francisco is even deeper into his laptop as Phyllis and Amber, in jeans and a hoodie, enter left.

AMBER
(as she does her 360°)
They need help, Mom. Becca says people are volunteering from all over the country.

PHYLLIS
But you know nothing about Staten Island. You've only been on the ferry once.

AMBER
It's not Pakistan, Mom. We'll be home tonight.

PHYLLIS
Let's donate! You've got a closet full of good sweaters, designer jeans you never wear anymore—sort them out and I'll have somebody pick it all up.

AMBER
Mom, it's not the same.

PHYLLIS
It's generous. I'm sure they can use quality clothing.

AMBER
We want to offer physical assistance. It's a kind of solidarity.

FRANCISCO
(not looking up)

So do both.

PHYLLIS

Francisco, are you going? I'd be more at ease.

FRANCISCO

Are you nuts? I'm the only one around here with work to do. Why are you trying to talk her out of being thoughtful and kind. It's perverse.

PHYLLIS
(taken aback)

I'm concerned for her safety, that's why. She's never been on Staten Island.

FRANCISCO

Americans live there. Whole families of them.

Becca enters right in jeans, carrying the hijab.

BECCA

I decided against the burka. I think it might confuse people and just get it the way.

PHYLLIS

Becca—

BECCA
(to Amber)
Take your surgical mask. There's probably a lot of dead things floating around.

Amber pulls it out of her pocket, holds it up.

PHYLLIS
Becca, can't you find a less dangerous way to help?

BECCA
(a beat)
Well, I guess I don't see it as actually dangerous, Aunt Phyl. I mean it's just an outer borough, it's not—Pakistan. And they need volunteers.

FRANCISCO
Everybody craps on Pakistan.

PHYLLIS
And how do you propose to get there?

AMBER
(realizes)
There are no subways running downtown.

BECCA
Yeah. I don't think the buses are running either. Okay, we'll just walk.

PHYLLIS

You can't walk to Staten—look, if you insist on doing this, I'll call a car.

Amber and Becca exchange a look.

AMBER

Mom—

PHYLLIS

The driver can wait there and bring you home. We'll pack some food.

BECCA

Aunt Phyl, it doesn't feel right.

PHYLLIS

Why not?

BECCA

You can't arrive at a disaster in a limo.

PHYLLIS

It's safe.

FRANCISCO

Just hitch a ride. There's two of you.

BECCA

Right. Come on.

PHYLLIS
What?

BECCA
City people are doing that, Aunt Phyl, helping each other get around.

PHYLLIS
Oh no.

AMBER
Mom, there's two of us.

PHYLLIS
(moves towards hallway)
Hitchhiking is forbidden in this family!

She stretches out her arms.

FRANCISCO
Jeezus.

Richard enters left, adjusting a camera strap.

RICHARD
What's going on?

FRANCISCO
A blockade.

                    AMBER
We're volunteering, Dad.

                    RICHARD
Hey, stepping out.

                    PHYLLIS
On Staten Island!

                    RICHARD
Good for you, Amber.

                    PHYLLIS
They are not hitchhiking to Staten Island.

                    RICHARD
Hitchhiking?

                    BECCA
Do you ever do volunteer work, Uncle Richard?

                    RICHARD
Well, I'm involved with a number of organizations.

                    BECCA
I mean physically show up—with your actual body.

                    RICHARD
Let me think.

AMBER
There are marathoners there, Dad, they stayed to help.

BECCA
Come with! New perspective, change of pace.

RICHARD
Thank you, girls, but—I'm intent on taking a long walk.

BECCA
Walk around Staten Island, it's paved. Establish some humanity credentials—I mean aside from philanthropy.

PHYLLIS
Becca, that's not—

BECCA
Sorry, I didn't mean it to sound negative.

AMBER
You could drive us, Dad. That's a terrific idea.

RICHARD
(with a look at Phyllis)
I'm sorry, I've got a lot on my mind right now.

BECCA
Uncle Richard, just—move your mind over, and leave it here for a while. I mean maybe it would help to step outside yourself and carry wet sofas from place to place, you know?

AMBER
And bring one of your cameras—a small one.

FRANCISCO
(ironic)
Practice your art.

PHYLLIS
We can't let them hitchhike, Richard.

RICHARD
(struggling)
Tell you what, I'll get the car out and drive you girls over the bridge. Then maybe I'll walk around on my own—or not. I'll reserve that decision.

BECCA
Deal! Let's hit it.
(fist bumps him)

They move for the hallway.

FRANCISCO
The Great Compromise of 2012.

AMBER
(excited)
Bye, Mom!

> *Phyllis waves, concerned. Just before they exit, Becca pulls the hijab over her face and Amber puts on the surgical mask, simultaneously. They exit with Richard.*
>
> *Phyllis turns for the bedrooms.*

FRANCISCO
Phyllis, can I get myself another glass of that squeezed orange juice?

> *She nods, points to the kitchen. He gets up to go as she's about to exit.*

PHYLLIS
(stops, turns to him)
Has anybody ever suggested that you grow up, be more mature and act like an adult?

FRANCISCO
Everybody. All the time.

PHYLLIS
But that doesn't interest you?

FRANCISCO
Why should it? What's an "adult"? Being older doesn't make you better. "Act like an adult?" Why? So I can care about—possessions? Money? "Reputations"? Politics? I have no interest in acting like an adult—even if that means adults don't like me because I'm not "mature." Well, why give a fuck about that? What's ma-

turity, anyway? It's an excuse to pretend. And stifle what you really think so you don't "offend" other "mature adults." Then everybody can keep on being insincere. No thanks. I'll just stay the immature asshole I am. Which doesn't mean I don't appreciate your hospitality. I do. Does that answer your question?

                        PHYLLIS

Entirely.

                       FRANCISCO

Excellent.

She exits up left to the bedrooms. He exits left to the kitchen.

After a couple beats, Wolf and Rhoda enter right from the sauna in big, fluffy white robes, red-faced, feeling good. They stop and look around at the empty space.

LIGHTS DROP

SCENE FIVE

Late in the day. Wolf is at the bar refilling his sister's drink. He's had a few himself.

WOLF
(hands her the drink)
Your quilt idea? Dynamic, I'm very impressed.

PHYLLIS
(sips)
You are? Seriously?

WOLF
Shows large-scale, tribal thinking. Almost biblical. Mom would be touched.

PHYLLIS
I hope so. Sometimes I wake up, middle of the night—I'm—life is strange without her.

WOLF
To see her disease on fabric? Personalized? She'd be tickled.

PHYLLIS
Well, it's relatively small compared to my next, my newest concept.

WOLF
(drinks)
Which is?

PHYLLIS
(shakes her head)
Still in the formative stage.

He nods. A silence.

WOLF
Boy, this bourbon -- I'll tell you.

PHYLLIS
What made you speak to Richard about the condo? Really—he has so much on his mind.

WOLF
Well, I felt it was time to get him on board.

PHYLLIS
I hate being pushed.

WOLF
Phyl, it's been seven months, we've had these offers.

PHYLLIS
So what? Really. What's the rush?
(new thought, concerned)
It's not financial, is it?

WOLF
No no no. We're just stuck, and Richard has perspective.

Rhoda enters left from the kitchen with a platter and a drink.

PHYLLIS

Well—it's all about process.

RHODA

Phyllis, these cheeses look sensational.

She hands her glass to Wolf, who refills it.

What process are we talking about?

WOLF

Phyl was saying how selling the condo is a kind of process.

RHODA

She's right, of course it is. And what we should do, I think, is get at the root of that process.
     (points)
This is an amazing Stilton. Try it.

Wolf takes some. Gives her the drink.

So what part of the process do you think is holding you back?
     (sips her drink)
Some kind of—ambivalence?

PHYLLIS

Towards what?

RHODA
Letting go?

PHYLLIS
I see.

WOLF
(pours himself more)
I've had a lot of bourbon!

RHODA
You and Wolf loved your mother deeply. But if I may say so, I think what's confusing the issue is equating a dollar number with her value as a human being.

PHYLLIS
You do.

RHODA
(nods)
Let's say you received a condo offer that was double what you are asking. Would that mean her "value" as a deceased parent would be doubled? It couldn't be, so why should a lower offer be an insult to the "value" of her memory? Her memory can't be conflated into bricks and mortar, or dollars. To put it as simply as I can: Your mother is not an apartment.

WOLF
(amused, settles into a chair)
It still can be quite difficult to—to let go.

                        RHODA

If you love someone? Absolutely.

                        PHYLLIS

But you didn't have that problem, did you?

                        RHODA

You mean?

                        PHYLLIS

With your mother. Letting go.

                        RHODA
                      (surprised)

No. I didn't love her.

                        PHYLLIS

Well, I did. I loved my mother.

                         WOLF
                       (laughs)

Rhoda's mother—that's a horse of a different color.

                        PHYLLIS

So maybe you can't understand missing your mother, losing your mother, seeing your mother suffer and die.

                        RHODA

We steered clear of each other and we stopped causing ourselves further pain—adult pain.

PHYLLIS
Oh? Are you sure of that? Neglect can cause pain.

WOLF
"Bosoms And Neglect!"

RHODA
Meaning what?

PHYLLIS
You didn't see her when she was dying, did you?

WOLF
Was that a play we saw?

RHODA
(hesitates)
No. It would've been hypocritical to suddenly appear concerned.

PHYLLIS
But you're not calling me a hypocrite.

WOLF
I can't remember a thing anymore.

RHODA
You did what you felt you had to do—maybe because of how you interacted with her before she got sick.

PHYLLIS
Oh?

                    WOLF
Rhoda, is this—this doesn't sound beneficial.

                    PHYLLIS
And how did I interact with her?

                    WOLF
Wait, just—

                    RHODA
Objectively, I'd have to say—unkindly.

                    PHYLLIS
Is that right, unkindly?

                    WOLF
                (rises unsteadily)
I think this is becoming—totally—unnecessary.

                    RHODA
                (points at him)
Wolf, sit.
                (to Phyllis)
Okay. I'm sorry but this has to be addressed. It's been building steadily, building up like—like family pus—and it's got to be squeezed out.

                    WOLF
                (sitting)
"Family pus"?

PHYLLIS
And—you're the squeezer? Who made you the squeezer?

WOLF
What? What are you—

RHODA
If I'd been unkind...

PHYLLIS
Which means what, I'm the squeezee?

RHODA
...unkind and cruel to my mother—so cruel she'd phone her son at midnight, sobbing.

PHYLLIS
Mom called you sobbing?

WOLF
This is about enough, Rhoda.

PHYLLIS
About me?

RHODA
Then I'd have issues with guilt, too. But I didn't, and I don't.

WOLF
I cannot condone this behavior—this—interaction.

PHYLLIS

Guilt? My guilt?

WOLF

I've probably had too much to drink. Is it apparent?

PHYLLIS

So the condo offers arrive and the two of you sit in judgement on me, psychological judgement.

WOLF

Never!

RHODA

Yes. It's too obvious to ignore.

PHYLLIS

Oh, a real professional opinion.

WOLF

What—do you know what you're doing?

RHODA

That's right. And we've paid a price for it, too.

PHYLLIS

Oh really? What price are you paying?

WOLF
(wave of nausea)

Oh boy—

RHODA

The price of the goddam condo.

WOLF
(rises)

No—cease! Cease and desist!

PHYLLIS

So this is about money, why didn't you say so?

RHODA

Not everything is about money.

WOLF
(wobbly, tries to intervene, stops)

No no no! This is our family—we don't—

PHYLLIS

Well, when it's about money it's about money.

RHODA

Money means you're rich, it doesn't mean you're right.

WOLF

Do you hear me?

PHYLLIS
(moving towards her)

Plenty of fucking Democrats have money, they're just too embarrassed to admit it.

WOLF

Oh no—please.

RHODA
(in her face)
I'm not a Democrat. I'm a registered fucking Independent!

PHYLLIS

Ha! Liberals in hiding!

RHODA

Hiding? In hiding? You're talking about hiding?

WOLF
(emotional overflow)
You must stop this! We do not sink to—to this level.

RHODA

The Hadassa WASP talks about hiding!

WOLF

Oh god.

PHYLLIS

How dare you question my faith!

RHODA

Pretense! Pretense and hypocrisy!

                    WOLF
            (tries to get between them)
We do not! Sink to—to this level.

                   PHYLLIS
I converted!

                    RHODA
Ha! And good luck with that!

                    WOLF
    (desperate, grabs a bronze sculpture from its pedestal)
Stop this now! The two of you.

       They tune him in. Wolf raises the sculpture over his head.

Stop stop stop stop! Or I'll—I'll do something!

       Wolf starts waving the sculpture around like a weapon.

                   PHYLLIS
                  (panicked)
Not the Watusi!

                    WOLF
I will, I mean it!

       She reaches, grabs onto the sculpture. Wolf resists—they tug at it.

PHYLLIS
(her ten year-old self)
Give it to me, Wolfgang!

RHODA
(steps in, reaches for the sculpture)
The two of you: time out, time out!

PHYLLIS
Let go—it's on consignment!

Rhoda yanks the sculpture from them. Wolf and Phyllis tumble to the floor. He's half on top of her. Rhoda is left holding the sculpture.

RHODA
(looks at it)
The Watusi??

PHYLLIS
(to Wolf)
Get off!

WOLF
(starts sobbing)
Oh god, oh god—I'm a man of moderation.

PHYLLIS
(pushing him)
Get off me.

RHODA
(bends to comfort him)
Wolfie, it's okay. Calm down, calm down.

WOLF
A man of moderation.

RHODA
We got carried away. We just had too much alcohol.

Phyllis grabs for the Watusi. Rhoda, not letting go, lurches onto the floor with them. Phyllis pulls it away, clutches it.

Francisco enters right in a short, white bathrobe. He's unsteady on his feet.

FRANCISCO
(dazed, grabs onto a chair)
Jeezus—

WOLF
I'm a man of moderation—a man of moderation!

FRANCISCO
(wobbly)
Maybe I stayed in there too long.

WOLF
I might—upchuck.

Francisco faints.

			RHODA
		(sees him go down)
Oh!

> *Holding the sculpture, Phyllis struggles to her knees, sees him on the floor.*

			PHYLLIS
Francisco?

			AMBER'S VOICE
We're home!

> *Amber enters with Becca in filthy clothes, grinning. Seeing everybody down, their mouths drop open.*

			AMBER
Mom, why are you all on the floor?

			BECCA
		(seeing Francisco, sprawled)
Dude?

> *Wolf rises doubled over, hand on mouth. Becca moves to Francisco as Wolf rushes off right.*

			RHODA
Wolfie?

FRANCISCO
(dazed)
Am I late? Am I too late?

BECCA
Late for what? What's with the shorty bathrobe?

RHODA
Wolfie, we just drank too much.
(gets up, stumbles)
We'll forget what was said. I promise!

AMBER
Mom?

RHODA
(trotting after Wolf, off right)
I'm right behind you, Wolfie!

BECCA
(amused)
Look, she's running! What is going on?

PHYLLIS
(gets up slowly)
Bourbon. Bourbon and history.

Becca and Amber help Francisco into a chair.

FRANCISCO
How was the circus?

                    BECCA
                   (laughs)
The circus?

                   PHYLLIS
He fainted. Amber, where's your father?

                   AMBER
Garage.

                  FRANCISCO
Hey, you gotta try the sauna.

                   AMBER
It's really weird in here, Mom.

   Phyllis, dazed, nods, replaces the sculpture.

                    BECCA
         (laughs, an arm around Francisco)
How long were you in there?

                  FRANCISCO
An hour?

                   AMBER
He could've died.

                  FRANCISCO
Hey, I liked it.

                         AMBER
Electrolytes!
                    (exiting left, fast)
Hydration!

                         BECCA
"Downtown DJ Dies in Park Avenue Sauna."

                       FRANCISCO
It's super-relaxing.

                         BECCA
                      (to Phyllis)
Is my dad okay?

                        PHYLLIS
Your father was a terrible teenage drinker.

                         BECCA
He usually has like one drink a week.

                        PHYLLIS
He used to throw up left and right.

                         BECCA
He must've been really enjoying himself.

                        PHYLLIS
I wouldn't go that far. Maybe I'll—I'll get coffee.

Battered, she exits left as Amber hurries in with a large bottle of blue sports drink.

BECCA

Thanks.

She helps Francisco.

AMBER

Drink it slowly.

FRANCISCO
(looks at her)

Dude, you just walked straight in. You didn't do the three-sixty.

AMBER
(realizes, smiles)

I did. I just walked in.

FRANCISCO

And nothing bad happened, right?

BECCA
(pleased)

Right.

(nods)

You know, you look really—chalky. It's a good look for him.

AMBER

Pale and washed out? Maybe we should go to the emergency room.

BECCA
It adds to his mystique. He'll be fine.

FRANCISCO
No. No I think I'm fading—quick, massage my penis.

BECCA
See?

AMBER
(a beat)
Becca, aren't you worried about your father?

BECCA
He's probably just barfing.

FRANCISCO
Wolfman embraces the bowl.

BECCA
Suck down those electrolytes, dude.
(notices)
What's wrong, Amber?

AMBER
(shakes her head)
I'm worried about my father.

BECCA
Why?

Amber just shakes her head.

Oh. You mean—jail?

Upset, Amber nods.

Hey, really rich people don't go to jail. I mean it would be a major system fuck-up.

                      AMBER

They don't?

                      BECCA

It's unheard of.

Rhoda Enters Right, slowly shaking her head.

What's up with Dad?

                      RHODA

He's gargling.

                      (amused)

Ah, Francisco's alive.

Francisco raises his hand as Phyllis enters left with coffee mugs.

                      PHYLLIS

Hot coffee! More brewing.

                    RHODA
            (takes a mug, cool to Phyllis)
Thank you.

                    PHYLLIS
                     (sits)
I see the non-adult has revived.

                   FRANCISCO
I can't handle all this affection.

                    RHODA
Fainting, barfing, and we haven't heard a thing about the outer borough.

            Richard enters from hallway.

                    AMBER
Dad!

            She rushes to embrace him, holds him.

                    BECCA
It was like stepping onto another planet.

                   RICHARD
            (surprised by Amber)
Well. We had quite an adventure, didn't we?

BECCA
And everyone was so grateful—they kept handing us coffee, doughnuts, pizza!

AMBER
Are you going for a run, Dad?

BECCA
Amber was awesome.

RICHARD
Run now? I'm kind of spent.
        (to others, re camera)
I've got some great shots.

BECCA
We helped this really nice family, the Chicolinis, shovel out all their wet stuff, and then Amber started feeding stray animals.

AMBER
I think you should run, Dad.

RICHARD
You do?

AMBER
You've got to stay in shape.

BECCA
In five minutes she was surrounded by dogs and cats. She was like the Pied Piper of Kibble.

AMBER

Yeah, it was kind of strange—the animals, all the debris, so much awfulness. But I felt like—I was okay with it.
(surprised)
I was really at home inside this—calamity.

PHYLLIS

I bet you could all use a nice hot shower.

AMBER

I think I'll investigate my Jewish heritage.

PHYLLIS

Really?

RHODA

What a terrific idea.

PHYLLIS

Because of the debris?

AMBER

I felt connected to people, something—other than Creamy. I liked it. That feeling.

Wolf enters right, in a white robe. He dabs his mouth with a washcloth.

WOLF

Don't worry, I'm fine! I'm fine everybody. Nothing to worry about. It's out of my system.

Wolf drops heavily into a chair as Phyllis hands him coffee.

Ah, gracias. Oh boy, my head's just pounding. Well, how was the disaster?

                    RICHARD

Take a look.
          (coming over, hands him the camera)
I was really in my element.

                    PHYLLIS

Good for you, sweetheart.

                    RICHARD

So many artistic opportunities—truly amazing visuals.

                    FRANCISCO

Any visual suffering?

                    RICHARD

Suffering?

                    FRANCISCO

Through the lens. Capture any suffering?

                    RICHARD

Sure. There's a few in there, but I didn't have my best equipment.

                    FRANCISCO

It's not in the equipment, dude.

RICHARD
Well, Candy Rocks, I'd say with today's technology an artist can practice at a much higher level.

FRANCISCO
Art's in your bones, it's your DNA. It's who you are, not who you want to be. What you're talking about, and I'm not saying there's anything wrong with it, just call it what it is—it's your fucking hobby.

RHODA
Francisco, for god's sake.

BECCA
He's opinionated, Mom, just like you.

RHODA
I'm sorry, it's not a license to insult! I don't voice every opinion I have regardless of people's feelings.
(realizes)
If I can help it.

FRANCISCO
That's because you're an "adult."

RICHARD
No. He's not wrong. I get carried away. It's really just an escape. I'm afraid that's all it is. An escape.

PHYLLIS
You take wonderful photos, Richard.

BECCA

Everybody needs to escape sometimes, Uncle Richard, right?

AMBER

We're going back Monday.

PHYLLIS

You are?

BECCA

You could bring a bigger lens, Uncle Richard—enlarge your escape.

RICHARD

I'm going down to the office Monday, but thank you.

BECCA

Skip it! You're the boss, right?

PHYLLIS

Are you sure you want to do it again, girls?

AMBER

Mom, they need help. We weren't the only ones.

RICHARD
(to himself)
It won't be pleasant at work, that's for sure.

BECCA
Hey, it was amazing. I mean we're in this house, sloshing around in wet, ratty muck and I look up and Amber's smiling at me!

RICHARD
(to himself)
I could skip it.

AMBER
(laughs)
You were smiling, too!

BECCA
Aunt Phyl, there were lots of college kids, it felt really safe.

AMBER
Yeah, not many grown-ups.

BECCA
I think the older you get the less flexible you become.

PHYLLIS
Yoga is so important.

BECCA
I mean psychologically flexible.

FRANCISCO
I'm inflexible, rude, and opinionated.

BECCA

Dude, those are your assets!

PHYLLIS

Wolf, a little something on your stomach?

Wolf raises a hand in resistance.

RHODA

Some dry toast is good.

WOLF

My mother always said that.

RHODA

Everybody's mother said that.

AMBER

Grandma had a lot of sayings, didn't she?

WOLF

She had wisdom.

Rhoda raises an eyebrow.

WOLF
(tearing up)
It's ridiculous—but I really miss her when I'm not feeling well!

PHYLLIS

She made you soup.

> WOLF

Delicious, homemade soup!

> RHODA

From a can.

> WOLF

It was from a can? I think I'll shower.

Rhoda and Phyllis nod.

> BECCA
> *(starts off, stops)*

So what's happening with grandma's condo?

A pause.

> PHYLLIS
> *(decisively)*

We'll accept the next offer.

Wolf and Rhoda look up, delighted.

> BECCA

Great. We can really use the money, right, Dad?

> WOLF
> *(flustered)*

Well it's not the—I'm—

                          BECCA
                        (surprised)
That's what you've both been saying for weeks!

                          RHODA
Phyllis, it's a splendid decision.

                          BECCA
Why not just say it? It's the truth.

                         FRANCISCO
Adult social terror.

                          AMBER
I might start to travel. Maybe even soon.

                         PHYLLIS
Wonderful! Travel where, sweetheart?

                         RICHARD
We've been trying to get her abroad for ages.

                          AMBER
Tanzania.

                         PHYLLIS
In Africa?

   Richard and Phyllis look at one another.

FRANCISCO
It's the Staten Island of Africa.

AMBER
For the elephants. Becca thinks I can volunteer there with a nonprofit.

PHYLLIS
In Africa?

BECCA
It could be a real career path.

PHYLLIS
You hate the zoo. Working with elephants?

AMBER
And rhino. They'll be extinct if the poaching keeps on. Dad, let's go for a run.

RICHARD
(brightens)
Really? Together?

PHYLLIS
Rhino?

WOLF
I might need three aspirin.

AMBER

We should start stretching, right?

RICHARD
(nods)

You know, I could skip the whole damn week, take photos and not go to the office at all.

FRANCISCO
(points at him)

Hey, psychologically flexible older person.

RICHARD

Join us, Candy Rocks?

FRANCISCO

Me? Go for a run?

RICHARD

Loosen up, dude. Step outside your comfort zone.

BECCA
(enjoying this)

Go for it, Rocks. Exercise!

AMBER

You've been sitting around all day.

FRANCISCO

It's my form of exercise.

AMBER
Dad's got extra sweats and T-shirts. I'll get my sneakers.

FRANCISCO
I almost died, remember—electrolytes?

Amber runs off left.

It's gonna take a lot more than a T-shirt.

RICHARD
Look, a psychologically inflexible younger person.

PHYLLIS
Really.

FRANCISCO
Hey, just run together. One-on-one. She's really upset you might go to prison.

PHYLLIS
What? He is not going to prison! You have no business saying that!

RICHARD
(taken aback)
It's a possibility, Phyl.

PHYLLIS
(upset)
Richard, please.

Francisco raises his hands in innocence.

RICHARD

I couldn't tell how tuned in she was.

FRANCISCO

Amber doesn't miss a beat.

BECCA

You should've seen her talking to strangers, trying to comfort people. It was amazing.

Amber trots in with sneakers, carrying a T-shirt and sweats which she hands to Francisco. He puts them down as if they were hot.

PHYLLIS

Maybe we should discuss dinner.

WOLF

I only hope I can sleep without pain.

RHODA

Anything works, Phyllis. We're easy.

WOLF

There's an old saying, I can't remember exactly, but the morning after, when you wake up with a terrific hangover you're supposed to take another drink, moderate in size, of exactly what you'd been drinking the night before. And it cures the hangover. I forget the saying.

The house phone sounds. Richard crosses to it.

BECCA

I'm showering.

She starts off left.

RICHARD
(turns to them from intercom)

Do we know somebody named Chicolini?

A silence. Becca has stopped.

AMBER

Oh!

BECCA

They made it.

AMBER

We invited a family. They lost everything—their house, their clothes, their rabbit.

BECCA

Wow, I didn't think they'd actually come.

PHYLLIS

A family? Here?

AMBER

There's only three of them, Mom.

RICHARD
(dazed, into the house phone)
Okay, send them up. Thank you.

BECCA
Francisco and I can move in with Amber. They're really nice, Aunt Phyl. We met people today who travelled from all over to help. Just dropped their lives because strangers were hurting. Total strangers! The runners stuck around, upstate people, out-of-state, local firemen, church people, teenagers. It was awesome.

AMBER
They were going to a shelter, Mom. We'll do all the work.

PHYLLIS
Oh.

BECCA
There was such spirit! We all have a chance to do so much good. And what does it take, really? And they kept thanking us! We just lifted disgusting objects and carried them from one dump to another. It wasn't hard. I mean it was easy doing it together, and it felt good, it felt right. We have all these opportunities, all these things we can do!

Amber nods. Rhoda is moved by her daughter.

FRANCISCO
(grins)
Dude, that is such total bullshit.

                    BECCA
                   (laughs)
Shut up!
                (impatiently)
Mom, what are crying about?

                    AMBER
We should change the sheets.

                    BECCA
Let's hit it.

She and Amber exit left.

                    PHYLLIS
                  (stunned)
The Chicolinis are in the elevator.
           (shakes her head in disbelief)
I better call Rosa.

She beckons for Rhoda to help her in the kitchen, and the sisters-in-law exit left, together. Richard starts his stretching. The doorbell rings. He looks up. Blackout.

                  THE END

SHADES

A Play in Two Acts by David Epstein

SHADES

was produced in an earlier version at the South Coast Repertory theatre in Costa Mesa, California. It was directed by John Frank Levey, with the following cast:

Lou-Ann Butcher	Kerry Noonan
Moonlight Meade	Michael MacRae
Bobby Fugazy	Randy Rocca
Andy Lowell	Sean Coleman
Natalie Konigsberg	Terry Hanauer
Dee Ryder	Eileeen Seeley

Act One

In the darkness, ripping fabric rends the air.

LIGHTS rise on a basement apartment on the west side of Manhattan, just off Central Park. Night. Rain splashes against the two half-windows upstage which are level with the sidewalk. A rag plugs a leak in one of them. From outside the streetlamp bounces color through the grimy panes dropping an orange-yellow glow into the room.

There's an old sprung rattan couch facing out stage left, a television placed in front of it. A beat-up club chair is angled into the corner beside the couch, a wooden crate before it serving as an ottoman.

A clean, neatly-made double-bed is up right against one wall. Across the room is a large mattress on the floor with blankets, no sheets. Near the mattress is a space heater on a long extension cord, glowing orange, facing downstage.

The kitchen, up center, has a small sink, a microwave, a two-ring hotplate, and a minifridge on the floor. A clean white towel hangs on a hook.

A sliding bathroom door is downstage right. The front door is down left leading up and out.

Three metal folding chairs around a card table are in the down right corner. On the table is a bunch of wild flowers in an old wine bottle.

There are lamps around the room. An old bureau, a battered suitcase, duffle bags are against a wall.

Overhead pipes lace the low ceiling; hooked from them on hangers are shirts, jackets, jeans.

Standing next to the table is HARRY "MOONLIGHT" MEADE, a weathered bear of a man over forty with long hair and a blue bandana rolled around his forehead. He's in faded jeans, desert boots, and a plaid workshirt. His rugged, pleated face has an American eagle intensity about it, softened by deep good humor and boyish energy. MOONLIGHT is in the process of arranging two dozen pair of sunglasses into long, neat rows their cases beside them. A hand-painted sign of a pair of sunglasses is on a piece of plasterboard resting against the card table.

Watching him is LOU-ANN BUTCHER, around twenty. Her slim body is tucked into jeans and a turtleneck, covered by a green sweater that's much too big for her. Her sweet, vulnerable face seems to hover between sadness and despair so that when she smiles it's like night lightning at sea. Her deep-set eyes and broad mouth belong to the face of a child who has become a woman, unannounced. She's fixed on what Moonlight is doing with the sunglasses. He finishes arranging them and takes a step back.

SHADES

MOONLIGHT

One more time?

(Lou-Ann nods)

I know you can do it. Just let her rip!

He walks around the room and approaches the table as a customer.

LOU-ANN

Sunglasses, mister?

He shakes his head, starts to walk away.

LOU-ANN

Hey, step right up! I got 'em—sunglasses!

He looks at her, signals her to wait, then walks around the table, stops, approaches casually as if checking out her wares. She watches him approach, look at the sunglasses, stroll right by. He turns, raises an eyebrow.

LOU-ANN

How about sunglasses? Real good price!

MOONLIGHT

How much?

LOU-ANN

Ten bucks?

He shakes his head, turns.

LOU-ANN
And eight! These are the eight ones.

She grabs at a line of glasses, knocking a few off the table.

They sell for two-hundred at Saks and Bondorfs, Polo, Bergmans ... all over!
(giving up)
Dammit, what in hell is the name of them stores, anyway?

MOONLIGHT
(reaches over, helps straighten the glasses)
It's a good start, Lou-Ann.

LOU-ANN
Don't humor me, Moonlight, I screwed up. I'm goin' to bed.

MOONLIGHT
You screwed up, but you'll be right on the money in the morning.

LOU-ANN
I might be gone. Just—outta here.

MOONLIGHT
We're gonna make a fortune, you and me. Startin' tomorrow.

LOU-ANN
I might. Before you're awake. I swear it!

MOONLIGHT
(grins)

Every night you say that. Every mornin' I gotta pull you up by the hair.

LOU-ANN

I will. I've got a plan . . .

MOONLIGHT

Somethin' powerful's at work in this room, Lou-Ann. Right in this little damp part of the world. You can't deny it, ever since you walked in.

LOU-ANN

. . . Nothin' can stop me. Nobody can.

MOONLIGHT

What we have here is a going concern, you understand me? And tomorrow we're cashin' in.

LOU-ANN

How can you be so sure of that?

MOONLIGHT

Have I been wrong since you've known me? How many weeks has it been now?

(waits)

Last time I was wrong was two-thousand eight. I picked Romney. Somethin' about his jaw. I didn't see how the American public could turn away from a jaw like that. It seemed to override the issues.

(considers)

If I have one weakness it's for a strong jaw. Every young woman I've had the pleasure of droolin' on had a granite jaw. That's a fact. Some men stare at the legs, or the breasts, some enjoy the beehind. Me? I've been a jaw man my entire virile life.

(smiles)

And do you have any idea what my favorite movie might be? Would you like to hazard a guess? Come on, be brave. Take a chance.

LOU-ANN

Moonlight, I am bushed. I don't want to play another game.

MOONLIGHT

You can do it! One time. I'll give you one guess, one guess and that's it. Come on, give it a whirl. One guess. Be my hero. What's my favorite movie?

LOU-ANN

Jaws.

MOONLIGHT

Tootsie.

LOU-ANN

Moonlight!

MOONLIGHT

(laughs)

But it was a good guess.

An educated guess!

(grabs for her)

He gets her, they're both laughing.

You rouse my thumpin' heart, girl, straight through to the soles of my feet, makin' every stop along the way.

They embrace.

I'm gonna make you rich. I'm gonna show you America day after tomorrow. I'll buy you food so thick and creamy you can't eat but a spoonful. I'll set your sweet butt down in a steamin' hot tub. I'll take you from zero to sixty in no time flat. Wrap you in clothes too fancy to wear.

(nods)

You and me, Lou-Ann. It's our shot. You watch. It's gonna be the biggest goddam demonstration march in human history, goin' from New York to D.C., and almost every one of them "Rescue the Constitution" people will descend upon this city tomorrow morning without sunglasses! There's gonna be over half a million of 'em across the street right there in Central Park, all worried sick over the country. How many of 'em do you think remembered to bring shades? Packin' all their "Save The Con" T-shirts and signs and shit, you think they gave one second's thought to their eyes? You know what the glare is gonna be like in that sheep-meadow bouncin' off the bandstand, tin loudspeakers, those aluminum scaffolds, and all? You got any idea? The only ones wearin' shades for certain gonna be the police. Okay, let's say a hundred thousand marchers remembered their sunglasses. Even some of them are gonna lose 'em or sit on 'em, right? That leaves four hundred

thousand without. Okay? Let's be generous now, let's say another three hundred and fifty thousand just aren't interested in sunglasses for personal reasons. What's that leave?
(pauses for effect)
We're talkin' about a potential market of fifty thousand people, Lou-Ann. Men and women with tired, fuckin' eyes.

She nods.

Ramon is droppin' off seven hundred knockoffs tonight—Ferraris, Porches, Ray-Bans, Calvins. I couldn't get any more.
(pats his shirt pocket)
That's every penny I've saved. If I can't sell seven hundred shades to fifty thousand squinting assholes then I don't belong in sales. I don't belong in marketing at all!
(confident nod)
When we set up out there at those two spots, we stand to walk back down here with six thousand dollars, cash money.

LOU-ANN

But why can't I work right beside you, like we been doin'?

MOONLIGHT

Visibility. Pure and simple market analysis. We need two operations.

LOU-ANN

I have never sold anything alone, Moonlight.

                    MOONLIGHT
Lou-Ann, with the glare hittin' off all the shiny baby-carriages, the flashy guitars, sun glintin' down on those shields and badges? Sweetcakes, those glasses are gonna sell themselves!

                    LOU-ANN
                    (hesitates)
You know it's rainin', Moonlight.

                    MOONLIGHT
Shut-up about that!
                    (hit by an idea)
Hey, hey—
                    (snaps his fingers)
Listen, listen I got it: You're a deaf mute!

He nods, she's looking at him.

You heard me! A goddam deaf fuckin' mute! The sympathy vote. They're all bleedin' heart types to begin with. You know any sign language?

She shakes her head No.

Well, don't worry about it. You were too poor. Your folks couldn't afford sign language. Good shit, what an idea! A goddam merchandizing *coup*. I don't believe I came up with this!

He does a little twist and shake of pleasure with Lou-Ann watching.

LOU-ANN

Moonlight?

MOONLIGHT
(looks up)

Huh?

LOU-ANN

You really want me to play deaf and dumb?

A flushing sound rattles the overhead pipes.

MOONLIGHT

You can't miss. Come on, let's give it a try. You want to act, don't you? You're aimin' for show business. Here's your first break.

The door to the bathroom slides open and BOBBY FUGAZY enters the room in pajamas, his head plugged into ear pods, looking at his cellphone. He's in his mid-twenties, with a pallid moon face, long, lank brown hair and a pair of granny glasses. He's about five foot seven with a body tending towards pudgy. He's got movie magazines tucked under one arm and a small red duffle bag under the other.

MOONLIGHT

Hey man, come on over here.

Bobby doesn't hear him.

Hey, Bobby!

Bobby looks up, not sure he's heard anything, smiles. Moonlight waves him over.

> BOBBY
> *(loud)*

What's up?

> MOONLIGHT
> *(whispers, points)*

Take the goddam ear things out.

> BOBBY
> *(removes the ear pods)*

Hey, what's happening? I couldn't hear you over Miley, she's sensational. What's up?

> MOONLIGHT

Lou-Ann's practicin' some salesmanship. Give us a hand.

> BOBBY

Far out. Sure. Sure. Hey Zendaya's building a house on some island somewhere, I just read it. Another house!

> MOONLIGHT

Be a customer.

> BOBBY

A customer? No problem.

He lays down his magazines and cellphone and then straightens his pajamas. He pats his hair, begins to clean

> his glasses, the red bag still under his arm. They watch him.

                              MOONLIGHT
                                (low)
Will you just walk past the fucking table?

> Bobby holds up his hand; he knows what he's doing. When he's ready he takes a spin around the room becoming a customer. He arrives, passing by the table when he's caught by the sight of the sunglasses. He approaches, nods to Lou-Ann and begins to examine the glasses carefully, tries a pair on, handles them, holds them up. Lou-Ann looks from him to Moonlight who signals her to stick with it.

                                BOBBY
                             (raises a pair)
What's the tariff?

> Lous-Ann turns to Moonlight, who offers no help.

                                BOBBY
Listen, I can't stand here all day. I'm due in court.

> Lou-Ann looks at the glasses, holds up five fingers, then three.

Eight bucks?
                          (looks around suspiciously)
Is it a secret?

Lou-Ann touches her mouth, shrugs.

BOBBY

You can't talk?

She nods, pleased. Touches her ear, shakes her head.

You can't hear either?

Lou-Ann nods again, smiles. Moonlight is watching this in disbelief. Bobby gets emotional.

Not deaf and dumb?

She nods.

Oh lord, that's dreadful, that's just a terrible thing. I knew someone once—oh god, I wish there was something I could do! Is there anything I can do? Wait—

He reaches into his pocket, hands her a wad of bills).

Take this, take everything I have!

Lou-Ann takes the bills awkwardly. She turns to Moonlight, who shrugs. Bobby takes her hand, holds it and kisses it.

BOBBY

God bless you.

He doesn't release her hand for a moment, staring into her eyes, looking for someone. Then he turns, puts on the sunglasses, picks up his cellphone walks slowly upstage, the weight of the world on his shoulders. He drops into the easy chair in front of the television. They watch him.

LOU-ANN
He's a real goofball, Moonlight.

MOONLIGHT
How much did he give you for the shades?

She looks in her hand, surprised, passes it over to him. He counts it.

MOONLIGHT
There's almost five hundred bucks here.

LOU-ANN
He could be in a B&B.

Moonlight walks upstage, passes Bobby the cash. Bobby hands over the sunglasses, staying focused on the TV the whole exchange. Moonlight returns to Lou-Ann, who has seated herself at the table, looking at her cellphone.

MOONLIGHT
I'd like to know what makes this boy tick.

LOU-ANN
I wonder how much money does he really have.

MOONLIGHT
(cleans the sunglasses with a cloth)
All he wants to talk about is movie stars and rock stars, television stars, over and over, stars and stars. He watches that damn box like it was wearin' a string bikini.

LOU-ANN
I never been in a B&B. I did stay in a motel once.

MOONLIGHT
(sits beside her)
He's been contributin', that's the fact of it. Ever since he got here—sweeps the stairs, real polite to the tenants.

Rain is coming down harder. Lou-Ann looks up.

LOU-ANN
You ever been in a trailer, Moonlight, when it rains?

MOONLIGHT
Trailer?

LOU-ANN
My people got moved to one, outside Logan after the dam broke. A real broiler. You could fry frogs on it in July. They're still sittin' there waitin' for a place. Been promised for two years.

MOONLIGHT
I had an old Airstream once.

LOU-ANN

Goddam state of West Virginia. You can hear it all. Rain hittin' off the roof like bullets.

MOONLIGHT

Me and my rotten wife. We pulled that old dinger all the way from Elco, Nevada behind an eighty-seven Chevy pickup. From behind it looked like a big spoon, you know? All curvy and silver.

LOU-ANN

Times I feel I could stab somebody in the neck.

MOONLIGHT

Young and in love. Every hundred fifty miles we'd pull off and crawl in the bunk for some old shaky-puddin'! Kept one eye on the odometer, one eye on the road, one hand up her skirt. I shouldda shot her when I had the chance.

LOU-ANN

Sounds like good times.

MOONLIGHT

I'd like to buy you somethin', Lou-Ann.

LOU-ANN

Greyhound to L.A.?

MOONLIGHT

Dark chocolate cake. Rub it all over you, lick it all off. Highly nutritious.

                    LOU-ANN
                    (grins)
You could get pimples.

                    MOONLIGHT
Worth the risk.
          (leans his head towards her)
I got you up the nose, no doubt about it.

                    LOU-ANN
                (touches his hair)
I appreciate that, I do. But I got dreams, Moonlight.

                    MOONLIGHT
Name one.

                    LOU-ANN
Los Angeles, Los Angeles, Los Angeles.

                    MOONLIGHT
They'll cut your throat and fuck you blind. I'd think twice.

                    LOU-ANN
You just don't believe I got it in me, do you?

                    MOONLIGHT
                    (rises)
I think you need a little seasoning is all.

LOU-ANN

You think since I wandered up here from Nowhere, USA, that all I'm good for is bein' your damn sales assistant, then rollin' with you at night.

MOONLIGHT

There is no call to be down on street-peddlin', it's an honest buck in the out-of-doors.

LOU-ANN
(nods towards the TV)

I've watched those shows, Moonlight. I can do that stuff. I'm not gonna be Lou-Ann Butcher my whole life.

MOONLIGHT

There's nothin' wrong with Lou-Ann Butcher.

LOU-ANN

She's nobody! That's the fact of it.

MOONLIGHT

I tend to disagree. And you're sure not gonna find her in L.A.

LOU-ANN

I gotta get out there, Moonlight.

MOONLIGHT

Fires and mudslides, Lou-Ann. It's just another place.

LOU-ANN
It's where you go if you're tryin' to be seen. I got a chance out there.

MOONLIGHT
(smiles)
The serious money's in New York.

LOU-ANN
(a beat)
You been real good to me, Moonlight. I don't know why.

MOONLIGHT
Hard to say. I been known to treat people like shit, too.

LOU-ANN
I keep tryin' to leave. I been outta here so damn many times.

MOONLIGHT
You're free to go.

LOU-ANN
I know that.

MOONLIGHT
Maybe it's my silver tongue keeps slurpin' you back beside me. Could be more goin' on down here than meets the naked nose.

LOU-ANN
You're twice my age, Moonlight! It's not healthy.

MOONLIGHT

Listen to your heart, Lou-Ann. Do you hear your heart sayin' "It's not healthy, it's not healthy, it's not healthy?" Hell no. Your heart is pumpin' blood. It's a muscle, it can't talk. That sweet heart is stimulating your little capillaries with red corpuscles. It does not have time to sit around and think. That's your mind sayin' "It's not healthy." And you know why? Because it's got nothin' better to do! Lou-Ann, your body will let you know when somethin' unhealthy is goin' on. You can trust your body. Because you know and I know and Sigmund goddam Freud knows that the mind is a dangerous fucking organ. And let's leave it at that.

Bobby yawns, changes channels on the TV. They look over at him.

LOU-ANN

How long's he gonna stay?

MOONLIGHT

Offer a man a bed you don't discuss dates. He's a puzzle with all them magazines, that red fuckin' bag.

LOU-ANN

He told me he was in a hospital.

MOONLIGHT

So what?

LOU-ANN

A ward.

MOONLIGHT

What kinda ward?

LOU-ANN

Well, I don't think it was maternity.

MOONLIGHT

So he's comin' off some hard times. Who isn't? No reason not to help a fella out.

LOU-ANN

He was in there a couple years, till they decided he wasn't dangerous. They let him out on the street.

MOONLIGHT

My daddy kicked me out when I was still in school.
(pause)
He was a brutal man, my daddy. He used to butcher hogs all day long, come home with blood under his fingernails, smellin' raw and meaty. Then he'd whack everybody around, eat, fart, fall asleep. His style was all whack and chop.
(pause)
My mother was more cut and slice. I wish she had been a saint like I heard so many mothers are. She just had a long, thin stream of mean runnin' through her.
(looks over at Bobby)
He botherin' you?

She shakes her head No.

MOONLIGHT

Somethin' about him, almost like havin' a dog around, you know? Kinda nice and homey. I like to try and figure a person out before I let loose of 'em.

LOU-ANN
(little smile)

You figured me out yet?

Bobby rises from his chair, stretches and comes downstage to his mattress. He looks over at them.

BOBBY
(cautiously)

How's it going? Big day tomorrow, huh? Main event, marchers from all over? They're saying even the U.S. Army could be called in here. Imagine that. Better catch a few Zs.

He begins to arrange his blankets, lays his red bag under his pillow.

MOONLIGHT

You do anything special today, Bobby?

BOBBY

The East River. It's quite a river. I walked all the way over there.

MOONLIGHT

No kiddin'?

BOBBY

Well, I've seen the Hudson. You can't go wrong with geography. I mean once you get a fix on a place, then it's a lock, you know? Even—even if you don't go back for years.
(beat)
There's benches all along the East River. People jogging, police all on alert, tugboats, cripples... hey I saw a guy in an electric wheelchair? Twelve-volt battery strapped in the back. You don't go real fast. I mean it's not dangerous or anything.
(nods)
How about you guys, anything special?

MOONLIGHT

Nothin' like that.

BOBBY

Well, it's quite a city.

LOU-ANN

You buy anything, Bobby?

BOBBY

Just beef jerky. And I had a Snickers for dessert.
(remembers)
Hey, tomorrow night? Chili. My treat. Three for eight dollars. Cans. I saw them on my way home. Unless your guys can't handle chili. I mean if you detest chili, if you despise it, then I'll pass it up. It does tend to explode on some people. But if that's the case then I'll just pass it up, no problem. I mean I suppose I've seen enough goddam chili in my life!

(looks at them)
So, do you care for chili?

MOONLIGHT

I'm good.

LOU-ANN

Me too, sure.

BOBBY

Unanimous!
(smiles)
I knew this fella in Grand Central Station, he would've done anything for a bowl of chili. I mean he was friendly, he was generous, but not about chili. We got to know each other hanging out in the terminal, the waiting room? On the benches. Those benches! Talk about uncomfortable. Anyway, we got to sharing stuff, whatever, and I kept noticing he'd vanish, disappear around eleven every night, you know? Gone. I'd be camping out. Next morning around rush hour, there he was panhandling again.
(shakes his head)
So one day we're working on coffee and jelly doughnuts and I brought it up about his disappearing. He looked at me kinda funny, like he was making a decision. That night he told me to follow him. I couldn't figure out where we were going. Talk about down! He had discovered this place below the trains. I mean another level. It's where the steam is, the boilers, those huge ducts and stuff? That's where he lived. It was real warm. That was the best part of it. There was a group down there, but they never spoke to each other. They talked to themselves, you could hear their conversations all alone. But they shared this secret. If too

many people heard about the place, forget it. It would've been overcrowded, a regular slum. So they kept it quiet. Some of them fixed up their spots with calendars, photos of loved ones long gone, President Kennedy, Marilyn Monroe, that sort of thing. They'd climb out to make a living during the day, come back down at night. Plus the rats. Fearless, you know, size of cats. You bang on a pipe, keep them moving.

(sees them listening)
I stayed down there a while, sure. It was okay, kinda cozy. Anyway, one night he starts talking to me about chili. And he gets this look in his eye. I've seen that look, it makes me nervous. He tells me about all the best places in America for chili, and how he's been to each one of them and he's in New York now doing research on Eastern U.S. chili, big-city chili. He swears by hot Texas chili but he likes sweet chili, too, like northern California chili. He's going on getting real excited about chili and then all of a sudden he reaches under his stuff and pulls out a gun with a silencer on it. He says I can't tell anybody this but he's been shooting immigrants up on the platforms, picking 'em off. He said that and chili are what he lives for.

(pause)
He didn't seem like a liar, you know, but I didn't look into it. I moved out. It got too hot down there. But I wonder how could he tell they were immigrants?

(shakes his head)
It's a funny thing about chili, some people just crave it.

Silence, they're lost in the story. A KNOCK on the door startles them.

                        LOU-ANN
The sunglasses!

                        MOONLIGHT
                   (moves for the entrance)
Ramon, my man!

> *He opens the door. Two college kids, NATALIE and ANDY in jeans with packs on their backs are standing there wet, cold to the bone.*
>
> *NATALIE, dark-haired, sturdy, and attractive has a fierce intelligence about her; she wears large, fogged-up glasses. ANDY is a wholesome American boy, gangly with a lopsided smile. He's carrying a "Save The Constitution!" sign.*

                         ANDY
Hello there! Boy, are we ever glad to see you.

> *Moonlight just looks at him. Andy reaches a hand and shakes with Moonlight who registers nothing.*

                        NATALIE
                  (cold, tired, matter-of-fact)
Natalie Konigsberg and Andy Lowell. We met you at three this afternoon outside the park on a bench. You gave us this address and said we could crash tonight if we got cold. We got cold.

MOONLIGHT
The college kids! Down from Massachusetts to rescue the Constitution.

ANDY
That's us!

LOU-ANN
Moonlight, they're freezing, bring 'em inside.

MOONLIGHT
Come on, come on. Our humble dump.

He ushers them into the room. Bobby watches them enter. He's very taken with them.

MOONLIGHT
This is Lou-Ann, and over there's Bobby in his pajamas who's stayin' with us.

LOU-ANN
I'm just stayin' here myself.

MOONLIGHT
Well, let's just unwind, sit down. Lay a little college on us, whatta you say?

Bobby flashes them the peace sign as they approach the table.

                    LOU-ANN
Some rain, huh?

                    MOONLIGHT
It's gonna stop!

                    ANDY
It stopped already.

> *Moonlight shoots her an I-told-you-so.*

                    MOONLIGHT
Sit down, sit down. Hey, I grabbed some flow-throughs from the market. Kitchen's still open.

                    NATALIE
Tea. God, yes. Thanks.

                    MOONLIGHT
We got water right here, cups, the whole shootin' match right at my fingertips.

                    ANDY
Listen, I can't tell you how much we appreciate this. Really.

> *They've taken seats at the card table. Moonlight moves to the hotplate. Bobby approaches carrying the glowing heater on its extension cord.*

BOBBY
(sets it up, aiming at them)
Forty BTUs. The thermostat's shot but the fan's good.

NATALIE
Gracias.

LOU-ANN
I got some dry clothes. They're clean.

NATALIE
Oh, bless you. Thanks.

Lou-Ann goes for her suitcase, grabs some clothes.

ANDY
Boy, did it pour out there! We didn't have a ground cloth or anything. Our sleeping bags are drenched—wet goose-down, man!

LOU-ANN
(carrying over the clothes)
You slept in the park? I almost did that once. Just after I got here. That's where I met Moonlight.

MOONLIGHT
Right off the bus. Like red meat in a tank of piranhas. Now she's got a home.

LOU-ANN
Just temporary. I'll be goin' west.

NATALIE
(undressing)
Dry clothes, thank you so much!

She has removed her sweater and undoes the buttons on her shirt. Bobby's eyes are jumping out of his head as she pulls the shirt off and stands there in her bra. He reaches down for the heater, lifts it, and aims it directly at her mid-section. She begins to unbuckle her jeans.

BOBBY
(holding the heater up)
GE product. Real solid piece of equipment.

Natalie starts putting on Lou-Ann's clothes. Moonlight grabs a shirt from an overhead hanger and drops it in Andy's lap.

MOONLIGHT
Dry and stiff with character.

ANDY
Hey, you folks are really super. It's great how a crisis can bring people together, isn't it?

Lou-Ann nods, tries hard to keep from looking at Andy, getting shirtless. Bobby, serious look on his face, holds the heater up aimed at Natalie in her underwear as she dresses.

ANDY
(puts on the shirt)
Hundreds of thousands gathering right there in Central Park all with one common belief: Save the republic, rescue the constitution!

NATALIE
He just ran for student council. Thanks.
(signals Bobby to put down the heater)

MOONLIGHT
Were you his campaign manager?

NATALIE
I was his opponent. I figured if you can't beat him, fuck him.

Moonlight roars a laugh. Bobby and Lou-Ann are dazzled by them.

ANDY
Natalie, for goshsakes.

NATALIE
Listen to him, "goshsakes." Who'd ever think he could fall for a socialist who doesn't shave her legs?

Andy laughs.

LOU-ANN
Really? You don't shave your legs?

NATALIE

I shave nothing! I wear thick glasses and my name's Konigsberg. It will stay Konigsberg. People who hide who they are make me puke. I don't need contact lenses or smooth legs to make me attractive. Ask him.

Andy grins, nods.

LOU-ANN

It sounds like the two of you don't have a whole lot in common.

NATALIE

The only things we have in common are politics and heavy sex.

MOONLIGHT & BOBBY

Hot dog!
Holy toast.

NATALIE

Is everybody marching tomorrow?

LOU-ANN

We'll be there!

BOBBY

Me? You kidding me?

ANDY

Good! Nobody has the right to suspend the U.S. Constitution. Nobody.

                        BOBBY
Hear hear!

                     MOONLIGHT
                (moves to the bathroom)
'Scuse me, folks, I gotta go caucus.

           He exits into the bathroom.

                        BOBBY
I spoke to my old man about this, this whole Constitution problem. He's a do-gooder, well-wisher, always thinking about the other guy, the underdog, always ready with the helping hand, a real scumbag of a guy, you know, a sweetheart, but I'm working on him.
                        (nods)
I'll break his neck one day!

      They're all watching him. He nods, turns to Andy.

                        BOBBY
                      (calmly)
So, where in Massachusetts you from?

                        ANDY
Peabody.

                        BOBBY
I been there. I been there.

ANDY

No kidding.

BOBBY

Sure, Holiday Inn right near town. Just a regular Holiday Inn, golds and browns, you know, every other room. Princess phone and all. Crummy, nice little town, Peabody.

Natalie checks her cellphone. Moonlight enters in a ratty old bathrobe.

BOBBY

You ever been there, Moonlight? Peabody, Mass.?

MOONLIGHT
(thinks)

Peabody, Mass. Peabody, Mass. I passed through once, I believe. In my guitar days.
(smiles)
Girl name of Amanda, bright blue eyes, hair like a field of wheat in the sun. Scar across her chin, right here. Young American beauty. I was on the move.
(shakes his head)
I remember her bendin' over one morning to pick up a barrette she dropped. All of eighteen.

NATALIE
(lifts a pair of sunglasses)

What's all this about?

LOU-ANN

We're gonna make a killing tomorrow!

ANDY

At the rally?

MOONLIGHT

That's right. Some of us aren't *in* college.

LOU-ANN

There could be a terrible glare. Aluminum and all?

NATALIE

You're selling these?

MOONLIGHT
(smiles)

You folks got somethin' against free enterprise?

ANDY

Not me.

NATALIE

Not Andrew Cabot Lowell. He's from free enterprise.

MOONLIGHT

And are you the little "commie infiltrator" we been hearin' so much about?

NATALIE
People have to make a living. It's just a shame they're forced to stand on street corners to do it.

MOONLIGHT
Shame? Hell, I love street corners.

BOBBY
Hear hear.

MOONLIGHT
There is nothing in god's good world to compare with standin' on a wide American avenue in broad daylight, sun beadin' a little sweat down your spine, sellin' your wares to John Public. Where I grew up people factory-worked day after day, hard labor they felt in their knees and backs. So they'd go get wrecked in the men's room smokin' a squiff and forget to bolt the exhaust to the chassis.
(passes the tea to Lou-Ann who serves the mugs)
I was a fuckin' roadie, Jack. I travelled. I saw this country. I tasted real food that was local-made like scrapple and grits and black-bottom pie. Stuff that people touched, you understand me, not processed shit that's wrapped.
(getting into it)
I drove around in old cars that never got recalled. We're talkin' fat Buicks and long shiny Oldsmobiles, eight goddam cylinders runnin' high-test, bodies strapped in *chrome*—chrome was style and grace. I'm talkin' about honest labor, which is why I'm out on the street. I got nothin' to hide, nothin' between me and the goddam public. No boss stickin' his hand in my pocket, no one degrading me. That's the American dream, goddam it!

ANDY

Amen to that.

MOONLIGHT
(drops a couple of packets on the table)
Now, who wants some artificial sweetener in their tea?

Andy smiles, takes a packet, empties it into his mug.

LOU-ANN

I bet you got a whole lotta friends marchin' tomorrow.

ANDY
(sips tea)
Half of New England, I guess. We're meeting up, then going down to D.C. together.

NATALIE

If we make it.

LOU-ANN

Whatta you mean?

ANDY
(tired of repeating it to Natalie)
Natalie knows it is illegal to call in the U.S. Army *domestically*—on its own citizens.

NATALIE
(tired of hearing it)
And Andy somehow ignores the fact that criminals are running the government.

ANDY
It's all going to be peaceful.

NATALIE
They're dangerous! They're stealing the country.

ANDY
Natalie's a pessimist.

NATALIE
I'm a *realist*.

MOONLIGHT
(moves upstage)
Well, I sure do like a place cracklin' with young pussy and good spirits. Make yourselves to home now. Lou-Ann, will you get tired soon, honey?
(points to the bed)
Headin' south everybody, big gig tomorrow.

ANDY
Hey, thanks again, Moonlight. Sleep well.

MOONLIGHT
Goodnight, sweet kids! You are all welcome in this humble house. Tough bein' a family man with no family. We shall never sleep

under a common roof again, but tonight we sleep as one. Happy hunting!

LOU-ANN
What about Ramon with the sunglasses?

MOONLIGHT
Ramon knows how to knock. Moonlight descends, everything ends, till tomorrow.

He lowers himself into bed.

BOBBY
(pacing, stops, picks up a magazine)
They say there's going to be a lotta top-flight entertainers coming. *Top-flight.*

NATALIE
(quietly to Lou-Ann about Moonlight)
Is he good to you?

LOU-ANN
He roars but he's a gentle man at heart. He's been real kind to me.
(points to the mattress)
I slept there the first couple weeks. Then one night—I moved. Sometimes he wakes up shriekin'. It's from the war; he saw action. I'm afraid it's gonna hurt him when I leave for L.A.
(pause)
He sings to me every night. Tells me a story.
(with a look to Andy)
So how long have you two been together?

ANDY

One semester.

NATALIE

Where are you from?

LOU-ANN

I'm from West Virginia, originally.

ANDY

Did you come for the march?

LOU-ANN

No. I came to escape.

NATALIE

Escape what?

LOU-ANN

Oh, just about everything, I guess. Family problems. We got wiped out a couple years back. Minin' dam burst up top of the mountain. Black water came barrellin' through the holler. Tore up every town, everybody for miles.

NATALIE

I read about that.

LOU-ANN

Really? Well, it just came with no warnin'. The company said it warned the people, but they lie, there was no warnin'. Black water rushin' down the road. I heard my daddy shout, "Get up, get outta the house, the dam's broke! Get up the hill!" We ran, my Mom and me and my sis.

ANDY

What about your father?

LOU-ANN

He was behind us, carryin' that boy of ours. I saw my daddy's mouth open, I guess he was screamin' but I couldn't hear him for the roar, and the next thing—he just disappeared. Under that sludge.

(beat)

That's the last time I saw my daddy. They wouldn't let me down at the schoolhouse with the bodies. Some of 'em got so ripped up. They did find Daddy but nobody could say for sure was it Duane. He was tore in half. If it was him.

(matter-of-fact)

My daddy was a big man, a real strong man, but when he gave you a hug, well that was gentle. And he could carry a tune, every time.

(pause)

They put us in mobile homes. We got mice and rats, roaches all around.

(shakes her head)

My mom started up with this man that lost his whole family a mile up the holler from where we used to be.

(looks at them)

You ever been to West Virginia?

They shake their heads, No.

LOU-ANN
It can be real pretty. If you like mountains.

Silence. Natalie and Andy don't know what to say.

BOBBY
(comes over carrying a newspaper)
It's in all the papers. Big names right out here in Central Park. They're all flying in, John Legend, Billie Eilish, Beyonce, Taylor Swift, Shamboozle, Oprah, Bono, Shailene Woodley, sure. Mostly from the coast.

ANDY
(looks at his cellphone, to Natalie)
Dee's going to meet us at ten-thirty. Her movie's finished.

NATALIE
(not thrilled)
Terrific.

BOBBY
First class, that's how they travel. You think they're gonna fly economy and get bothered by people? And those narrow seats? Forget it, baby, first class.

ANDY
We're invited to the wrap party in Brooklyn, at Flaubert.

NATALIE
Pass.

BOBBY

I mean these are people who have done stuff, they *exist*, they've accomplished things.

ANDY
(looks up)

This tea is perfect.

LOU-ANN
(gazing at him)

It's just regular tea.

BOBBY
(tuning in)

Dee? Dee who? A wrap party? Not Dee Ryder? She's in college in Massachusetts, isn't she?

NATALIE

She's in our house. She just took a semester off to shoot a movie. It's a unique arrangement, she has a two-week out-clause for all her classes.

BOBBY

In your house? Dee Ryder is in your house?? Holy toast. She's stupendous. I mean for someone her age and everything? Dee Ryder is phenomenal. What accomplishments, what credits!

LOU-ANN

You know her? God, she's gorgeous.

BOBBY
(pacing)
She's on the map! *The* map! Ho-lee toast.

LOU-ANN
I saw her in *Spendthrift,* then on a talk show in the same week! I read all her interviews. I wonder how in the world do you get so beautiful?

NATALIE
She's not any prettier than you are, Lou-Ann.

LOU-ANN
No! Beauty like that? Beauty like that is . . . is superior! It's *noticed.*

NATALIE
She's just a regular person with a fancy job.

LOU-ANN
She is not a regular person! She's *glamorous.* There is nothing "regular" about her.

NATALIE
She has bad breath.

LOU-ANN
What?

Lou-Ann stares at her in disbelief. Natalie nods.

BOBBY

So Dee Ryder's meeting up with you guys tomorrow.

NATALIE

Bring your Clorets.

ANDY

(looking at his cellphone)

We're all meeting at 53rd and Broadway, northeast corner. Then we march up here together into the park.

Natalie puts her head down on the table and closes her eyes. A silence.

BOBBY

(shakes his head in wonder)

Dee Ryder. Holy toast.

LOU-ANN

I bet she remembers her sunglasses.

(looks at them)

Bobby, why don't you let them crash on the mattress? Look how beat they are.

BOBBY

Sure. No problem.

(picks up his red bag)

Hey, you guys can have the bed. Go ahead. I'll take the chair. It's a great chair. I love it. I don't know a better chair.

                    NATALIE
                (raises her head)
It looks big enough for all three of us. Andy?

                    ANDY
                    (rising)
Looks like heaven to me.

                    BOBBY
Holy toast . . . Okay, no problem! I'll be right there.

> Natalie and Andy go to the mattress and drop down, exhausted. Bobby paces holding the red bag to his chest. He keeps glancing over at them, excited.
>
> Lou-Ann turns out the light over the card table and walks upstage to where Moonlight is asleep. She kneels by the bed, clasps her hands together and begins her prayers.
>
> Bobby circles the room. He does an involuntary jig of excitement.

                    BOBBY
Dee Ryder. Just like that!

> He stops pacing, comes to a halt at the mattress where Natalie and Andy have dropped off.

Smiling and happy, he aims the heater towards them. He unzips his red bag and removes an apple. In three ravenous bites he demolishes the apple, staring down at the couple. The heater glows.

Upstage, Lou-Ann continues to pray.

BLACKOUT

END ACT ONE

ACT TWO

The following day.

The bed is made; the other mattress piled with blankets. Two sleeping bags hang from an overhead pipe, drying. The card table is gone but the chairs that surrounded it remain. Strong sunlight drops into the room through the street-level windows. No one is around.

From outside we hear VOICES moving through the streets into Central Park. Some are call-and-response CHANTING: "Save Our Constitution!/ We The People!/ Save Our Constitution!/We The People!" Others are SINGING: "This Land Is Your Land/This Land is My Land . . . "

(Note: At moments throughout the act, singing and chanting are heard in the distance as waves of marchers roll into the park.)

Just outside the door there is a loud thump! Something clatters to the ground. After a moment the door is flung open and a card table sails into the room, crashes into the chairs.

Moonlight enters, steaming. Lou-Ann, annoyed, follows, lugging a second card table and the sunglasses sign. She leans them against the couch.

MOONLIGHT
Goddam cockroach sonofabitch!

(kicks a folding chair)
I've spent my whole life goin' the extra mile, trustin' in man, turnin' the other cheek, givin' people the benefit of the doubt. I have the patience of a goddam saint! Why the hell didn't you check those boxes last night?

LOU-ANN

I did check. I told you—

MOONLIGHT

The top layer! It's the oldest scam in the book. He saw you comin' out the front door and switched boxes.

LOU-ANN

You wouldn't wake up.

MOONLIGHT

How hard did you try?

LOU-ANN

I didn't put a knife in your ear! He's bangin' on that window, you're snorin', they're all sleepin', it's rainin' up there again. I bring up the cash and then he's screamin' in Spanish to hurry up! He pushes these boxes at me, grabs for the money—two creeps in the back of the van are makin' noises at me like I'm a piece of chicken!
(imitates their sounds and gestures)
And now you're yellin' at me for not bein' more careful.

MOONLIGHT

That's right. Once you pulled the cash outta my pocket it was your show. I'm judgin' you on your performance Lou-Ann, and you blew it!

LOU-ANN
(pauses)

I'll pay you back.

MOONLIGHT
(sits, pulls out some cash)

I know. When you make it big in L.A. That'll be just about when this place goes co-op.
(starts to count the cash, disgusted)
We sold every piece we had in forty-five minutes.
(passes her cash)
Here.

LOU-ANN
(hesitates before taking it)

What's this?

MOONLIGHT

Don't argue about it! Just because you screwed up doesn't mean you haven't worked your butt off every day. Hide it from me.
(stands)
Good shit, we'd be rollin' in it right now, wouldn't we? Did you see 'em, blinded by the brilliant sun, bumpin' into each other, trippin', fallin' down, smashin' into sharp objects. I felt like a goddam oasis. They were crawlin' up to me one by one, shieldin' their red fuckin' eyes with one hand, wavin' cash with the other—

pleadin' for protection from the awful glare. Lines of people dependin' on me and I fuckin' ran outta product!
(looks at the cash)
Four hundred and fifty bucks.
(shakes his head)
Do you have an idea how many business ventures I have been associated with in my lifetime? Do you?

As he lists them he gets hotter and hotter as if each one had a villain.

Used cars. Used furniture. U-Drive. Interior design. Beer delivery. Landscaping. Cooking. Tires. Driver's Ed. Garaging. Haulage. Dumping.
(pause)
Fish! Snakes! Music!

LOU-ANN
Cooking?

MOONLIGHT
That's right. I was a fuckin' chef in a small Chinese-American restaurant in Watervliet, New York. I did the American. And I was good! They closed the place down because some asshole choked to death on a shrimp roll! Every single damn thing I've tried has dried up on me, but that doesn't mean shit. Who the hell wants to lead one life? I just hate gettin' ripped off. It took me eight months to put that cash away.
(pause)
I'll tell you I have faith I have in this country. I fought for this country but if there's one thing I've learned it's everybody fucks

over everybody else with rare exception, that's the American way. Be rich or be nothin'!

                    LOU-ANN

Maybe we could find him.

                    MOONLIGHT

Find a five-foot eight-inch Hispanic with curly black hair, brown eyes, a niece ass, and a thin mustache? That's everybody in Spanish Harlem including the women. Forget it. We can't go on a cockroach hunt, it's too late.

                    (resigned)

We just gotta pick up and start over again. One more fuckin' fresh start.

                    (deep breath)

Lou-Ann, what a man seeks in life is a triumph. Just one moment when he can throw his fist up in the air because he's *done* it, whatever the hell the thing may be.

                    (nods, paces)

And the sonofabitch is *elusive*, but it's out there, and it's inside, too, deep in a man. He might struggle his whole life searchin' for that one moment. Every man worth a damn hunts it from the time he's a boy with his baseball bat and sometimes you don't ever get it. But that's the gamble of bein' a man. And if that thing hits, the explosion that follows is called a goddam personal triumph!

                    (looks at her)

I promise you, Lou-Ann, somethin's gonna click for me. I got plenty of time and low overhead. There's money out there on the goddam street that the average sucker can't even see. Money waitin' to be harvested and *bushelled*. All you need is energy and a positive attitude in this country and sooner or later it all falls in your lap. Believe me, I'll command respect. I'm gonna be a rich goddam man one day.

LOU-ANN

When this place goes co-op?

MOONLIGHT
(a hard look)
You shouldn't wise-off at me, Lou-Ann.

Demonstrators move into the park singing, "... Sweet land of liberty/ Of thee I sing/Land where my fathers died/Land of the pilgrim's pride..."

LOU-ANN
(hears the singing)
Moonlight, let's go back there!

MOONLIGHT

Shouldn't razz my ass cause you know what I'm capable of? I'm capable of lovin' you till death do us part.

LOU-ANN

Have you ever seen so many people in one place bein' so *committed*? Everybody marchin' up the avenue, holdin' signs, holdin' hands, pushin' babies, kids on daddy's shoulders, old ladies sailin' in wheel chairs, wavin' their constitution banners, people singin' together, dancin' to the conga bands right past the soldiers!

MOONLIGHT

Smokin' dope, pickin' pockets, grabbin' ass—

LOU-ANN

It was brotherhood, Moonlight, just like he said last night.

MOONLIGHT

Everybody high on life. You liked that boy, didn't you?

LOU-ANN

He had a real nice smile.

MOONLIGHT

A college boy bein' abused by a horny co-ed is not exactly up against life, Lou-Ann.

LOU-ANN

I was jealous of 'em—all the future they got.

MOONLIGHT

Girl, you've got more raw future in you than those two'll ever dream of. What you got they don't hand out in college. It comes from *within*, and don't you ever forget it.

LOU-ANN
(pause)

You ever done drugs, Moonlight?

MOONLIGHT
(what a question)

Lou-Ann, there was a time in my life when I was doin' so many different drugs that the pharmacy used to call *me* for a prescription.

LOU-ANN
Come on, let's go back. They'll have speeches and music and stuff—like a county fair!

MOONLIGHT
You expect me to go back there after what I just been through? You know how many empty cases I opened while they're all standin' there watchin'? Then one joe college in a goddam "Eat Me" T-shirt starts to snicker. A goddam college snicker. Before I know it they're all laughin' at me with my empty cases! And you want me to go back and join *in*?

LOU-ANN
There was only six of 'em.

MOONLIGHT
I'm tryin' to tell you somethin'.

LOU-ANN
They'll all be blended in, lost in the crowd.

MOONLIGHT
Listen to me. I'm . . .

LOU-ANN
You won't even recognize 'em!

MOONLIGHT
. . . I'm ashamed to be seen, godammit!

LOU-ANN
(hesitates)
But you got nothin' to be ashamed of. It was just a business venture gone wrong.

MOONLIGHT
Don't you hillbillies know the meaning of humiliation?

LOU-ANN
(stung)
Humiliation? You think you know about that?
(shakes her head)
I lived in a tin can for two years with a phony stepfather always managin' to be present when it's time to get undressed. I used to wake up with his fingers inside me, kneelin' by my cot!
(breathing hard)
You been embarrassed out there and I'm sorry for it, but that's not what I call humiliation. Now come with me. We gotta shake this thing off.
(watches him, turns for the door)
Suit yourself.

MOONLIGHT
You forgettin' somethin'?
(points)
That cardboard piece-a-shit suitcase and every rag you own.

LOU-ANN
Well, how about if I just leave it all here so you can have somethin' to sniff me by? Forward my mail care of L.A.

She turns for the door picking up her shoulder bag.

                    MOONLIGHT
                      (beat)

Lou-Ann! Lou-Ann?

She hears something in his voice that sounds like fear and she hesitates. He moves towards her.

                    MOONLIGHT

Whatever you think is out there?
                    (shakes his head)
They snort young girls up off the street. You think maybe with a few bucks in your pocket you're all set, but you're a piece of honeydew, Lou-Ann, and out there everybody eats melon.

She moves to go.

                    MOONLIGHT

You know I'd die before I'd let anyone mess with you.

She stops.

                    MOONLIGHT

You'll never find a man who appreciates your spirit and your youth. Young boys like that can give you a big laugh and a hard squeeze. Young boys'll heat up the soles of your feet and make your neck stiff. But I'm offerin' you a home. I'm offerin' you *protection* and trust—and the secret desires of a grown man.

He's beside her. She's staring up at him, the certainty gone from her face. He drops to his knees, puts his arms around her.

From outside, CHANTING: "Save Our Constitution!/We The People! Save Our Constitution!/We The People."

She hesitates, finally pulls away from him, turns and exits. He rises, starts to go after her—stops—as she backs into the room, a look of stunned disbelief on her face.

Coming in after her is a young woman in faded jeans, a jean jacket and a Yankee baseball cap. She's got a 35mm camera over her shoulder. DEE RYDER has the clean, healthy good looks of a scrubbed child. Right now her large, hazel eyes, wiser than her years, reflect an inner terror she is struggling to contain.

Behind her is Bobby, the red bag draped over one arm. When they have entered the room, he kicks the door closed and tosses the red bag on the mattress. In his hand is a small pistol, a Ruger LCR. His face is flushed with excitement, sweating. He smiles, suddenly lets out a string of ringing Whoops!

BOBBY
Eeeyaa! Ya! Ya! Eeeyaa! Ya! Ya!

Lou-Ann gapes at Dee Ryder, who is frozen. Moonlight is alert for anything. Bobby, gun in hand, waits for a reaction.

Outside, the CHANTING marchers move into the park.

(Note: In what follows, the gun is raised or pointed only when Bobby feels threatened or issues an order.)

      BOBBY

So? So?
      (laughs)
Huh! Tell me about it, huh!

      MOONLIGHT

Bobby, why don't you lower that before you blow your nose off?

      BOBBY

That's it? That's all you got to say? I'm talkin' Dee Ryder. I'm talkin' star-time right here in your place. Royalty, Moonlight! This is American royalty—what the hell kind of greeting is that?

      MOONLIGHT

Well, I'm real impressed, Bobby. Sincerely impressed. Of course.
      (to Dee)
How do you? It's a pleasure.

  She says nothing.

      BOBBY
      (lowers the gun)
That's more like it.

MOONLIGHT
Say, why don't you folks start walkin' and we'll catch you for drinks at the Sherry Netherlands! Just give us a few to spruce up and we'll join you. My treat!

BOBBY
We came for a visit.

MOONLIGHT
Well, we're not exactly set up for company, Bobby. Hey, the Carlyle's got a nice piano-bar right across the park.

BOBBY
(notices the fallen table and chairs)
What the hell happened in here?

LOU-ANN
It's nothin'. Just a little crash.

BOBBY
Dee, I'm sorry to bring you to such a messy place.

MOONLIGHT
The Palm Court at the Plaza? That's a swell spot. I'll call for a table.

BOBBY
We're staying.

MOONLIGHT
Good decision! It's a pleasure to have you both.

LOU-ANN

Can I get you anything? We don't really have anything, but if there's something I can get you—

MOONLIGHT
(offering a seat)

Our best chair. Please.

(raises the card table, sets it up)

And we've got this table right here to go with it. Table and chairs, everybody's got 'em!

He pats the chair. Dee remains on her feet.

BOBBY

She'd rather stand.

MOONLIGHT

I believe it.

(beat)

Hey, how about some homemade tea? You must be thirsty what with the Constitution, the singin', marchin' and all. Lou-Ann?

(nods for her to get the tea but she doesn't budge)

I did a lotta marchin' myself once upon a time. Parris Island. Hell of a place to march.

(snorts)

Now the very word "march" makes me want to bite the head off a chicken! Those were the days.

DEE

What do you want with me?

A silence.

MOONLIGHT

Lou-Ann honey, that water's not gonna boil itself.

BOBBY

Dee, are you thirsty?

LOU-ANN

Bobby, what *do* you want with her?

BOBBY

Could you use a nice cup of tea?

Moonlight nods to her, subtly. She picks up on it and nods to BOBBY

BOBBY
(happy)

Terrific! Super. Tea all around. So we'll all sit down and—nope—give me your cellphones first! Hand 'em over.

They do. He pockets them. Lou-Ann, with a glance at Moonlight, heads upstage to the hotplate. Bobby pulls a chair out for Dee, beckons her to sit. Moonlight pulls up a chair and waits. Finally, she takes a seat. Moonlight sits. Bobby, pleased, joins them.

                        BOBBY
                  (conversational)
Hey, so how did you guys do with the shades? It's still pretty early. You must've sold out, right?
                        (to Dee)
They were hawking sunglasses at the rally, good equipment, first-class merchandise.
                        (to Moonlight)
So? Big bucks or what? Come on. You guys made a bundle, am I right?

                        MOONLIGHT
No.

                        BOBBY
Whoa! Okay. No more questions.
                        (to Dee)
Sensitive man, okay? How do you like your tea?

                        LOU-ANN
All's we got's some sugar.

                        BOBBY
That's what's *here*. We can get her whatever she wants. I mean if she likes milk, or lemon, or honey. That can be gotten, right?
                        (Lou-Ann nods)
Good.
                        (to Dee)
Anything you want, we'll get. How do you like your tea? Plain?

(Dee nods)
"Plain tea." It's traditional. There's style in that. It's English. Princesses drink plain tea, the guys too, the princes. Plain tea.
(pause)
So how did the shoot go? Sounds like a terrific cast.
(to the others)
She shot right here in the city. Great locations, sure. We were talking about it as we marched here. You should've seen the crowds. I didn't have any trouble finding her. Fifty-third and Broadway, just like they said, northeast corner, ten-thirty: Dee Ryder! I just slipped right in there beside her, people chanting and all, "Save Our Constitution!/ USA/ Save Our Constitution!/USA!" We walked side by side all the way up here, then just before we got to the corner over there I suddenly realized, hey, I might never see her again! So I just—I asked her didn't she want to drop by and say hello? And here we are.

> Dee shoots him a look. Lou-Ann carries over the tea. She can't take her eyes off Dee as she sits to join them. Bobby holds the Ruger down low.

MOONLIGHT
So now what? What are your plans?

BOBBY
Can't we have a nice cup of plain tea without everybody worrying about the future? I mean we're having tea with Dee Ryder. Let's enjoy it, for chrissake.

MOONLIGHT
Problem is, Bobby, we might not have us a future unless we start to worry about it.

BOBBY
(puts the Ruger on the table in front of him)
Moonlight, this is just between me and her. You've got nothing to worry about, believe me.

LOU-ANN
(to Dee)
Do you color your hair?
(Dee, incredulous, shakes her head)
I knew it! Me either. I think it's a mistake.

BOBBY
What's a mistake?

LOU-ANN
Coloring your hair. Natural beauty is the most prized. And that's what she's got, natural beauty. I can see that close up. Anybody can. That's what makes for glamour. L.A. is filled with it. Sunshine, casual dress, nothin' hidden. Everything right up front, out in the open. That's what so attractive about it. And she doesn't even wear eye shadow.

MOONLIGHT
Listen Bobby, I don't mean to put a damper on this nice tea party, but we might start thinkin' about the consequences of this— event.

Dee gauges the situation, sensing that Moonlight might be her ticket out. SINGING in the distance...

BOBBY

You just let me handle it, Moonlight. It's an under-control situation, here, all thought out.

MOONLIGHT

Right. Except this is my place. You understand me?

DEE

Excuse me!
(deep breath)
I am very scared. I want you all to know that and let me go. I would like to leave after tea. No one else will ever know anything about it. Ever. I hate to eat and run but I get the impression it would be the best thing all around, just a short visit.

LOU-ANN

Hey, we got nothin' to do with this—me and Moonlight.

DEE

That's fine! I can keep a secret. I won't mention a word to anybody.

BOBBY

Listen, Dee—I can call you Dee now, right? We're getting to know each other here, and I want to give you my personal assurance there's nothing to be scared about. I'm just out to be your friend, that's my aim here.

DEE
Okay.

BOBBY
Only I can't let you go. I mean—just—go.

MOONLIGHT & LOU-ANN
Why not?
How come?

BOBBY
(glaring)
Will you two stop bugging me! All I'm after is some cooperation. We've got a guest here who means—she means a whole lot to me. She is not just some *date*. I mean she's not just anybody coming over for tea. This is one fine human being and if you won't take my word for it—go to the movies! It comes right through, shines through every part she's ever played. There is a large, generous soul at work. I'm not talking trivial, mean-spirited bitches. This young woman is from class, the cream of America—and—and we're becoming friends here. This is the start of our relationship and I want it to start on the right note. We're not talking short-term.
(looks at Dee who nods.)
You see? You think I'm making this up? We've spent *time* together.

MOONLIGHT
I'm real happy for you Bobby, but this is my place. You understand me? And you have kidnapped a movie queen.

                            BOBBY

Don't say that, Moonlight—

                          MOONLIGHT

You have brought her home to papa. Now unless you like bein' tucked into bed every night by a tattooed gorilla, I suggest you start thinkin' fast, cause I been in the slammer, Jack, and soft meat like you is what they dream about.

                            BOBBY
                      (it begins to sink in)
What?

                          MOONLIGHT

That's what I'm sayin'.

                            BOBBY

But this is just friendly here—

                             DEE
                      (holds up a hand)
Wait, please. Nobody's going to jail. I will consider this a simple visit if you just let me go now. I've had a few scary moments, but it hasn't been so terrible and I'm ready to forget it ever happened.

                            BOBBY

Oh no, please, you can't just forget it. Please don't forget it.

                             DEE

I mean the bad parts! How could I forget the . . . the tea, and the conversation?

                        BOBBY
Right.

                         DEE
                    (slowly rising)
So we all agree.

> *Bobby is torn. Moonlight is fixed on him, and the gun. CHANTING outside, "Save Our Constitution/We The People!"*

                         DEE
A friendly visit? A nice cup of plain tea?
   (takes camera off her shoulder, hands it to Bobby)
I'd like you to have this.

                        BOBBY
          (eyes light up as he accepts camera)
Me? For me?

                         DEE
From me to you. Use it in good health.
            (edges towards the door)

> *Just as she reaches for the doorknob, there is a loud KNOCK. Everyone freezes.*

> *Bobby jumps up, motions with the pistol for Moonlight to go to the door just as it opens and Natalie enters talking angrily...*

NATALIE

The U.S. Army has *no* goddam business at a peaceful rally! It's—
(*stops, stunned*)
Dee?

DEE
(*just as surprised*)

Natalie!

NATALIE

What the *fuck*? I don't believe this. You're here? *You* are *here*? I mean what the *fuck*?

LOU-ANN

Hi Natalie.

NATALIE

I came for the sleeping bags, and to pee. Why are you . . .
(*sees Bobby with the pistol*)
. . . here. Oh shit.

BOBBY

Where's the guy?

NATALIE

The guy? Oh boy, I walked into a kidnapping. Andy! He's in the park. Oh boy. Oh boy, and we told you just where to find her.

LOU-ANN

She does not have bad breath at all. That was just a mean thing to say.

NATALIE

I apologize!

BOBBY
(beckoning)

Cellphone. Give it here.
(Natalie hands him her cellphone)

DEE

Well, I was just going.

BOBBY
(raises the pistol)

Stop.

DEE
(stops)

It's really great to see you Natalie. Did you give them my address and phone number, too?

BOBBY

You don't like her, do you, Dee?

DEE

Listen, I—

BOBBY

She's no good! You know what she was doing last night in bed? Teasing me! Rubbing up against me all night long while her boyfriend's fast asleep.

NATALIE

Oh, jeezus—

DEE

You slept with him?

BOBBY

Don't you deny it.

NATALIE

I'm an active sleeper, all right?

BOBBY

You're garbage.

NATALIE
(terrified)

I've known it my whole life.

BOBBY
(advances on her)

Worthless, no-good trash!

Natalie screams.

MOONLIGHT

Bobby—

Bobby swings around, gun flashing in the air. Everyone drops.

MOONLIGHT
(from the floor, quietly)
Could I please have a word with you?

BOBBY
(catches his breath, to the others)
Get up, move away from the door.

They do. He goes upstage with Moonlight to talk, his eyes on the three women.

NATALIE
(points to the bathroom)
Do you think... could I please?

BOBBY
You make me sick.

NATALIE
I know. I can't help it.

BOBBY
(points to Dee)
She's been here a lot longer than you.

NATALIE
And I bet she didn't go yet. Movie stars never do. Please?

BOBBY
Fast!

Natalie steps into the bathroom, slides the door shut. Bobby keeps far enough away from Moonlight to protect himself. As they confer—

DEE
(low to Lou-Ann)
Can you help me?

LOU-ANN
(low)
Of course! Just tell me, do you love L.A.?

DEE
L.A.? No, I don't. Listen, please—

LOU-ANN
You don't?

DEE
What does he want? Do you know?

LOU-ANN
What am I supposed to do with that?

DEE
Does he want money?

LOU-ANN
What? I don't know. We'll help you. I promise!

Moonlight and Bobby come downstage towards them.

BOBBY
Dee, I need to ask you a few simple questions.

The bathroom door opens and Natalie steps out pulling up her jeans. Bobby swings the gun towards her. Her hands go over her head. He turns back to Dee. Natalie buckles her jeans. Moonlight watches every move.

BOBBY
Is anybody waiting for you?

DEE
My sisters. But not yet. Afterwards.

BOBBY
Where?

DEE
A restaurant downtown. Nanning-Hunan.

NATALIE
That's great Chinese.

BOBBY
Quiet!

MOONLIGHT
What time are you meeting them, Dee?

DEE
Four. Then we all go to Washington. No one's looking for me yet.

Moonlight and Bobby exchange a glance. Moonlight nods to him.

NATALIE

May I ask what's the point of this? I mean is it political? A statement of some kind, kidnapping a symbol of America's perverted values? Because I can understand that, I—

DEE

Shut up, Natalie.

BOBBY

What is she talking about?

MOONLIGHT
(stepping in front of Bobby)

You know Natalie, I had nothing to do with this goddam mess but I would seriously consider ransoming your ass just for the fun of it.

NATALIE

You wouldn't get much I'm afraid.

MOONLIGHT

More than I got! Who the hell are you kids anyway walkin' around with money and cameras and a college education? What have you ever done except be somebody's kid!

LOU-ANN
(re Dee)

She works, Moonlight.

Works?

MOONLIGHT

BOBBY

She's a film actor!

MOONLIGHT

Baggin' groceries is work. Pickin' strawberries is work. Layin' brick is work!

(points to Lou-Ann)

She's worked harder the last three weeks than they've ever worked in their lives.

NATALIE

You're right. All we really do is take exams. It's embarrassing.

DEE

That's all *you* do. I came down here with a gun in my back trying to figure out what you people want from me. I've listened quietly, but I will not listen to your asinine opinions about my work! I've been getting up at five-thirty every morning busting my chops to be beautiful and fascinating till nine at night. I've had people doing my face and doing my hair, tugging at my clothes and shining lights in my eyes. I've had to play love scenes with a dumb hard-on who can't remember more than one line at a time and a director who wants me to sit on his lap between set-ups. But I am there because it is my job, and *nobody* is going to tell me it's not work! Now what are your goddam demands??

Lou-Ann and Bobby have been gazing at her in astonishment. Lou-Ann starts to applaud, stops.

MOONLIGHT
(calculated)
I want you and your girlfriend to get your butts the hell outta my house! Go ahead. I'm sick of spoiled kids complainin'—get out!
(moves menacingly towards them)
Go on! Go to Bloomingdales. Go take exams. I've had enough of the both of you.

They rush for the door, but Bobby leaps in front with the gun—

BOBBY

Stop!

They freeze.

BOBBY

I won't have anybody insulting Dee here, Moonlight. I mean it.

Moonlight shakes his head, shrugs; it hasn't worked.

BOBBY
(proudly)
You heard what she said. You heard how she said it? Now you see what I've been talking about? You see what I mean? It's not just anybody I'd ask down here like this.
(paces gun in hand)
You know, I've always wondered what it's like to be recognized on the street, respected. I mean what's it feel like to have talent, be praised, to be someone of stature in this country, you know? Revered?

He stops, seems to be lost in his thoughts a moment. Low, distant sounds of CHANTING: "Save Our Constitution/We The People!"

DEE
(quietly)
Bobby, what do you want? Will you tell me, please?

BOBBY
Hmm?

DEE
You don't want to hurt me. I know that.

BOBBY
Oh no. No no no.

MOONLIGHT
Bobby, Dee here's suggesting maybe if you told her your plans, you could help her, help her out. She needs your help.

BOBBY
(pause, looks up)
I want an interview.

MOONLIGHT
An interview.

BOBBY
Yes.

                    NATALIE
You want to interview Dee?

                    BOBBY
You shut your mouth around here or I will shoot you where you want it most! You understand me?

She nods fast.

                    BOBBY
I get interviewed by Dee! Dee Ryder interviews Bobby Fugazy, all right? Then, if I feel like it, I interview her. Is that loud and clear enough? My interview first.

                    MOONLIGHT
Loud and clear, Bobby, loud and clear.

                    DEE
What sort of interview should it be?

                    BOBBY
Real!
                    (beat)
A real interview. With . . . with an intro. My credits. Questions about my life, my backstory, who I'm supposed to be. And how I got here, where I'm headed. What's been going down with me lately and what's coming up next. My schedule. My plans. I want to be asked where I'm from, who my influences are. Witty, you know, with repartee and . . . and banter. Indelible memories and all.

(pause)
The whole thing. On record. Part of history, cameras, studio audience, commercials—real life.

DEE

Where would we do it?

MOONLIGHT
(indicating card table and chairs)
Where else but right here in the studio?

BOBBY
(nods, grins)
Exactly. Moonlight, would you handle the arrangements?

MOONLIGHT

Well, I was hopin' you'd ask.

BOBBY
(warning)

No moves.

MOONLIGHT

No moves.

BOBBY

And you be the emcee.

MOONLIGHT
(deep breath)
A role I was born to play. Now, let's see—

          (points to front door)
That door, that door is off-stage. That's what they call—

BOBBY

The green room.

MOONLIGHT

The green room. Each guest goes out there and waits in the green room...
          (shoots a look to Dee)
... just goes out, socializes, throws up, till their introduction. How's that?

Bobby nods. Dee nods. Moonlight grabs a large boot, pulls back a chair. He lays the boot on the chair.

MOONLIGHT

This here is the camera. It's a one-camera show.
          (points to another chair)
Dee? If you'll sit there in the host's chair. Thank you.
          (to Natalie)
You're in the way!

NATALIE
          (jumps)

I'm sorry!

MOONLIGHT

Use your imagination, for chrissake. Lou-Ann, the two of you are in the studio audience. Where's the camera? Where's the set?

Dee is seated at the table. Lou-Ann finds the right spot and gestures for Natalie to crouch beside her on the floor.

                    MOONLIGHT
All right! Ready to roll, Bobby.

Gun in hand, Bobby steps to the front door, pauses, goes out leaving it open a crack. He peeks back in, then moves out of sight.

                    MOONLIGHT
                    (low to Dee)
Stick with me!
                    (the Emcee)
Folks, our star guest is up next. We're real proud to introduce that charming, gifted, "crazy" young man, Mr. Talent himself: Bobby Fugazy!

He signals for applause from Natalie and Lou-Ann along with himself and Dee.

The door opens wide and Bobby strides in, transformed. He has removed his glasses, opened a couple of top buttons on his shirt, combed his hair. The gun is visible in his belt.

He walks to the table with a studied, DeNiro self-confidence. He nods with a little finger wave to the clapping audience, then leans over, takes Dee's face in both hands in greeting.

He salutes Moonlight with two fingers. Finally, he sits, crosses his legs. He takes the gun out of his belt and lays it on the table.

Moonlight crouches behind the "camera."

            DEE
    (a trouper under strain)
Bobby, welcome, welcome! Looking good. How long will you be in town?

            BOBBY
    (charming, another persona)
Thank you, Dee. I wish I knew. I'm never sure when I'm going to get called away—been living out of a suitcase seems like years.

            DEE
Just like vaudeville.

            BOBBY
You got it. A little of this, a little of that!

            DEE
You know, Bobby, people in our studio audience and across the country would love to know more about you, details to fill in the void, if you don't mind.

            BOBBY
Dee, that's why I'm here. Well, I was born in a small town in northern Pennsylvania called Turtle Creek, but we moved to Kansas when I was a boy.

He takes a pack of Marlboros from his shirt pocket, offers them around to no takers.

DEE

And Kansas was where you were raised? Your family?

BOBBY

You go it. Real hot and real flat in central Kansas!
(lights up)
My Dad struggled for a while, long hours, rubbing, cutting, buffing, scrubbing—I mean that man could buff. You talk about buffing, he buffed! Night and day, forging ahead, weekends and all, dirty laundry, one-dollar bills crumpled up on his bureau like bird-shit! But then zip-zap! Things kind of took off, you know? He made good. It came his way. Things worked out.
(beat)
He became self-made.
(inhales deeply)
Plenty of money. Jealous neighbors. Real kind of success story.
(begins circling the glowing tip of the cigarette above his palm)
Oh, I was well cared-for, don't worry about that. When I was a kid we had this nurse? She had one bad arm, one game leg, hard-of-hearing, and she was overweight, but she could do it, she could nurse! She used to hug me real tight and yell, "Bobby you can be anything you want in this state, anything at all!"
(pause)
One afternoon I came home from school and there she was, gone! Just vanished. No longer present. Thin air. Imagine that. Hard to believe, right, after all those years?

> *(little laugh)*

You ever try to get a straight answer from a self-made man? Would you like to know more about my parents, Dee?

> *They are all fixed on him. VOICES in the distance: "... My native country, thee/Land of the noble free ... "*

DEE

Yes, I would Bobby. Please fill us in.

BOBBY

Well, my mother was a real barracuda, you know? A total *bat*. Tall, skinny woman. But a fancy dresser. Designer quality, jewelry and all. Loves the jewelry. Lots of gold, heavy rings, big on the bracelets, silver broaches. You can hardly see any *skin*, you understand and there's a whole lot of ground to cover. So much cheap crap all over the place. And cosmetics: creams, lotions, tighteners, looseners, lighteners, darkeners—she loves to travel. I guess that's where I get my wanderlust, Dee.

> *(beat)*

I was what they call a "late child," you know? Full of hell—rodeos, videos, Carvels, cartoons, canteens, whatever. Back at the house I'd be kind of tough to handle, screaming, hurting myself, tossing stuff—breakables. It's a house with *objects*. Just hearing that sound of the mother's voice, that kind of broken-glass bat-screech of the mother and all—

> *(shakes his head)*

By then they were traveling all over, fact-finding, dining out, and here was this *kid*. I mean uncontrollable when they got home.

(pause)

So—I don't know, for my own good, just like that one day: Good Samaritan Hospital. Lockdown and all. Let me tell you about *that*.

(looks around at them)

Then, after a while they just thought for my own development, life-experience, you know, I'd be better off out on my own, on the road. See America? It's been a great education. I mean you can't beat America, it's all here: Paris, Kentucky; Rome, New York; Havana, Illinois; Venice, California; New London, Connecticut; Oslo, Minnesota; Oxford, Pennsylvania—

(laughs)

And you can do it all by bus!

(nods)

I have no regrets, Dee. It's been a great life.

(looks down at his hand, circling his palm with the cigarette)

But you see, every once in a while I'd be alone somewhere, in some motel somewhere—with walls—I really hate being alone and I'd wonder: why the hell does it have to be this way? I mean I never did anything but lose a few jobs, you know? I mean everybody loses a job.

(angry)

I mean who the hell never lost a damn job! Will you tell me that??

(shakes his head)

But who cares? And where do you start? I mean who the hell cares at all? That's what I can't figure out. No matter how hard you try, who gives a rat's ass? Nobody, right? I mean what's the point how great your accomplishments if there's nobody there to...to enjoy a CD with or go sailing with, you know? If you sail.

(looks at Dee)

Do you care, Dee?

                    DEE
                  (moved)
Yes, I do, Bobby.

> *He nods at her and then he looks down at his hand and he Pushes the burning cigarette into the palm of his left hand...*
>
> *He shudders, but makes no sound, holding it there. Dee gasps. Moonlight rises. Lou-Ann and Natalie, stunned, slowly get to their feet.*
>
> *Bobby picks up the gun. They all hold still.*

                   BOBBY
I believe you, Dee! I really do.

> *He laughs, then sobs begin to wrack his body. His head drops to his chest, gun-hand lowers. Moonlight motions for Dee to go, run! But instead she gets up and moves to Bobby.*
>
> *Natalie, seeing her chance, flits across the room and exits out the door..*
>
> *Dee looks down at Bobby's shaking body, then very tentatively touches the top of his head. He quivers. She strokes his head a few times and then gets down beside him on her knees. He's still holding the gun.*

                    DEE
Bobby? You've had bad times, terrible breaks. But it's going to be better. You can't stop trying. Things will get better.

                    BOBBY
                   (head down)
No. No, I'm ... no ...

                    DEE
People can be kind, you'll see. But you've got to keep caring about yourself.

                    BOBBY
                (looks up slowly)
I am nobody.

                   LOU-ANN
Oh no! No—

                    DEE
That's not true, Bobby. You are. You are a precious person!

> He stares at her. She reaches for his burned hand, brings it to her face. She looks at it and puts her tongue to his palm and holds it there.
>
> Bobby gazes at Dee, disbelieving what he sees and feels. Slowly, with trepidation, he touches her head with his gun-hand, tentatively as if it might be swatted away ...

MOONLIGHT
(to himself)
I'm gonna put this in my memoirs.

The smile of a little boy breaks across Bobby's face and for a long moment he is incandescently happy. The happiest person we've ever seen.

BOBBY
I'll be okay, Dee. Don't cry. Please don't cry.

She looks up at him.

BOBBY
Please don't be upset.

DEE
(holding his hand)
We've got to do something about this burn, its serious. It's a serious burn.

BOBBY
I know. We'll do whatever we have to do—from now on. I'll take your advice.
(gazes at her)
Holy toast!

MOONLIGHT
Bobby?

                        BOBBY
              (not taking his eyes from her)
What is it?

                       MOONLIGHT
If it's not too painful, if you're up for it I thought maybe now's the time to interview Dee. I mean while everything is so—peaceful, you know?

                         BOBBY
                        (to Dee)
Would you like to? I've have a lot of questions to ask. And we've got a lot of catching up to do. And the future.

           Dee glances at Moonlight, who nods.

                          DEE
Sure, let's do it, Bobby.

                         BOBBY
                  (holds up his hand)
Don't you worry about this.

                       MOONLIGHT
All right, let me do the intro.

                        LOU-ANN
Wait, just—

                       MOONLIGHT
Quiet!

BOBBY
(gets out of his chair)
Okay, I'll move over here.
(to Dee)
You get ready. This is great, really great! I'm okay, don't be upset now, really. It hardly hurts. I never felt better! Go on, go ahead.

Dee rises and moves slowly for the door, turning once to see how she's doing. Bobby is not watching her. Moonlight nods, urging her out. Lou-Ann holds her breath.

Dee exits, closing the door behind her.

LOU-ANN
(low)
I was only gonna say we got a can of Crisco for that burn. It'll *help*.

Moonlight puts a finger to his lips, silencing her.

BOBBY
Moonlight? I want to apologize.

MOONLIGHT
(gently, eyes on the gun)
Not necessary, Bobby.

BOBBY
Sometimes, you know, sometimes I jump into things before I've thought them through.

MOONLIGHT
You're doin' okay, Bobby. Gettin' sliced up like an orange, pieces of you cut off and stolen away. I been there myself.

BOBBY
I get caught up and excited and before I know it—whammo! Complications, anger, big problems.

MOONLIGHT
I'm not angry at you, son. We all get to feelin' a little disappeared at times.

LOU-ANN
Amen to that.

BOBBY
So even a friend, when I think I've found one—I zoom in! I mean that's my style, right? I'm just sorry for the commotion.

MOONLIGHT
I opened my door to you, Bobby. You got a home here.

Bobby hears him, nods. He points to the door for Moonlight to begin. SINGING drifts in from outside, "... For purple mountains majesty/Above the fruited plain... "

MOONLIGHT
(gathers himself)
Ladies and gentlemen, we've got a real celebrity here with us this afternoon, a young woman of the silver screen who has made a name for herself in such a short time, at such a young age. She's

on the map of America! Let's welcome that lovely lady of film and college, Miss Dee Ryder!

> *They all look at the door, waiting.*

> *Bobby signals Moonlight to say it again, louder.*

                MOONLIGHT
              (relieved, louder)
Let's all welcome Miss Dee Ryder!
              (Nothing happens.)
Dee? We're ready for you!

> *Bobby hesitates then motions for Moonlight to get Dee. Moonlight walks over, opens the door and peers outside. He turns back to Bobby and shrugs.*

                BOBBY
              (rising)
What??
    (leaps to his feet with his gun, rushes for the door)
Dee! Dee! Deeeeee come back!

> *He exits. A moment of stunned surprise.*

                LOU-ANN
That was the most exciting thing that's ever happened to me.

                MOONLIGHT
Let's hit it, Lou-Ann.

He grabs a duffle bag from behind the couch.

LOU-ANN

What? Moonlight, what are you doin'?

MOONLIGHT

(throwing possessions into the duffle)

Sweetcakes, we gotta git.

LOU-ANN

But they all left. What are you worried about?

MOONLIGHT

I'm worried about the man with the gavel, wearin' a black robe. Come on now—

LOU-ANN

But we didn't do anything.

MOONLIGHT

(keeps packing)

And that's called "not guilty." You get a chance to say that if you stay and wait. Deep in my heart I know I'm innocent. I don't find it necessary to say the words.

LOU-ANN

Dee wouldn't do that, Moonlight. She *cared*. She confided in me. She kissed his hand!

MOONLIGHT

But she didn't stay, did she?

LOU-ANN
(looks at him)
You don't trust anybody but yourself, do you?

MOONLIGHT
I believe you gotta save your own ass, is what I believe. Pack up!

LOU-ANN
I pass!

MOONLIGHT
We don't have time for bein' pouty, Lou-Ann. What's the matter with you? This place is *hot*.

LOU-ANN
I like it here! And I'm a damn hillbilly, that's what's the matter with me.

MOONLIGHT
I withdraw that unfortunate remark. Now come on, it's dangerous.

She crosses her arms defiantly.

MOONLIGHT
Okay. I'm gonna tell you somethin'. Ramon was settin' me up. Ever since I started doin' business six, seven months back he's been honest to the penny, waitin'. He got me trustin' him and I stopped close-checkin' a while ago.
(tough admission)
I never wouldda gone to the bottom of them boxes either.

LOU-ANN
So, you just feel like apologizin'?

MOONLIGHT
I'm bein' honest with you, goddamit.

LOU-ANN
And you'd walk right out on Bobby too, wouldn't you?

MOONLIGHT
No. No I am runnin' out on Bobby. I'm sorry for that boy but he's a ship breakin' up in a storm and shame on me for thinkin' it, but I just wanna get away from him fast as I can.

LOU-ANN
You go ahead and do that.

MOONLIGHT
(pause)
Lou-Ann, I know you don't wanna be sharin' a cell with a friendly older woman in a crew cut, crackin' her knuckles.

LOU-ANN
(hears it)
You can't scare me, Moonlight.

MOONLIGHT
Think of what's up there above us, Lou-Ann. We got this whole wide green country just waitin' for us to slam that door, climb them stairs and jump in. There's a gold mine of opportunity for a spirited man and woman. It's on every corner, in every town and

every city. You just gotta reach out there and grab it! Goddam I believe that.

(quietly)

I still believe it.

(pause)

I'll miss this dump too, but I'm ready for a real place.

LOU-ANN

Maybe this is as real as they get.

MOONLIGHT

(looks at her)

I wonder how did I live without you my whole rotten life? And how in the world will I live without you when you're gone?

LOU-ANN

You know, sometimes it's hard to say when you're makin' fun of me Moonlight, and when you're makin' love.

MOONLIGHT

(as he packs)

I've known some women in my life, Lou-Ann. And every once in a long while, if you're lucky maybe once or twice in your entire life you find somebody with the magnet in 'em. It don't matter how old you are or how old they are or the color of their hair. If they got the magnet in 'em you can't do nothin' but get pulled in. You know right off you're gonna make a damn fool of yourself, but you get *drawn*. And you gotta live it out.

(shakes his head)

And if they feel the magnet in you for *them*, well then that's *business*. Then nobody's walkin'. Then you're talkin' do or die.

(looks at her)
We got the magnets in us, girl!

He reaches, embraces her.

Upbeat voices are on the move CHANTING: "Save Our Constitution!/We The People!/ Save Our Constitution!"

LOU-ANN

Will you take me to L.A.?

MOONLIGHT

Well, there's nothin' like a fresh start to shake the frogs outta your pants.

LOU-ANN

You will? You'll do it?

MOONLIGHT
(grins)
I hear it's a big town for sunglasses.

LOU-ANN
(hugs him)
I just wonder is it everything it's suppose to be.

MOONLIGHT

Bless your heart for sayin' that. And if you don't like it we can always move. Naples, Florida?

She looks up, hearing another group move SINGING. She hurries to throw clothes in the duffle.

MOONLIGHT
(checks his wallet)

We got almost seven hundred bucks between us.

He picks up a paperback by his bedside, slips it in the duffle, zips it, lifts it over his shoulder.

Hollywood and Vine?

Lou-Ann, with a last look around the basement, takes his outstretched hand and they exit.

Outside the singing and chanting stop—there's a charged silence.

Voices become angry, confrontational:

"Save Our Constitution!/We The People!/Save Our Constitution!/We The People!"

A burst of AUTOMATIC GUNFIRE followed by SCREAMS.

More AUTOMATIC GUNFIRE. MAYHEM on the street.

Andy enters covered with blood. His right arm dangles. He glances around, staggers to a chair at the card table, drops into it.

SHOUTS, Yelling outside. Another round of AUTOMATIC GUNFIRE.

Enter Bobby carrying Dee in his arms. She's lifeless. Terrified, he stops in the middle of the basement, sees Andy slumped at the table.

Ambulance SIRENS are nearing the park.

From the street FRAIL VOICES rise up: "Save Our Constitution!/We The People!/Save Our Constitution!/We The People!"

LIGHTS BANG-UP FULL in a white-hot blaze.

Rooted in place, Dee in his arms, Bobby's mouth opens in a silent scream.

BLACKOUT.

THE END

To the Memory of Michael Roemer—
Extraordinary Filmmaker, Invaluable Friend

and Kevin Graham—
The Best of Us

Acknowledgments

FOR THEIR ENTHUSIASM and help along the way, my special thanks (in no special order) to:

>Tom Schwarz and Ellen Howe
>Richard Liebman-Smith
>Keira Naughton
>Jim Naughton
>Michael Posnick
>Dana Wallace
>Lonnie Carter
>Robert Montgomery
>Nancy Mette
>Kathy Graham
>Geoff Pierson
>Frank McDermott
>Janet McDermott
>Susan Raebeck
>Barry Raebeck
>Frank Coppola
>Robert Gold
>Paul Bresnick
>Barbara Strong
>Jay Strong
>Dan Lieberman
>and my worthy editor / publisher Karl Weber

David Epstein

About the Author

DAVID EPSTEIN'S PLAYS have been produced Off-Broadway, at regional theatres across the country, and abroad. He wrote the screenplay for the film *Palookaville,* which began life at the Sundance Festival, was honored at the Venice Film Festival, and opened in the United States and worldwide to critical acclaim. Mr. Epstein has written screenplays for the major movie studios, and his films have aired frequently on network TV and on PBS.

Mr. Epstein has taught at Colgate University, at NYU, and at Yale. He is a graduate of The Yale School of Drama. He lives with his wife Kate on eastern Long Island and Oahu, Hawaii.

MORE PLAYS BY
DAVID EPSTEIN

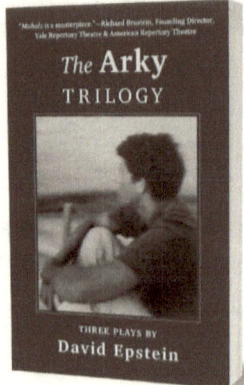

A series of three plays—**Mahalo, Desperados,** and **Arky**—tracing the story of an American family navigating a years-long crisis driven by a child's mental illness. By turns harrowing, wildly comic, and deeply affecting, **The Arky Trilogy** vividly captures the shocking twists of life as experienced by one family.

ISBN 978-1-953943-35-4 • $22.95

From a surreal musical satire featuring much-loved American rogues like Billy The Kid and Ma Barker to a bitter takedown of the Iraq War, these four plays (**Wanted, They Told Me You Came This Way, Mine,** and **Deceived by Colin Powell**) expose painful home truths about our nation's soul.

ISBN 978-1-953943-78-1 • $22.95

AVAILABLE WHEREVER BOOKS ARE SOLD
For a special price on the three-volume David Epstein collection,
visit www.rivertownsbooks.com

www.ingramcontent.com/pod-product-compliance
Lightning Source LLC
LaVergne TN
LVHW091618070526
838199LV00044B/849